Praise for *T*

M000298549

"It is rare to happen upon beautiful thoughts so beautifully expressed, but S.A. Snyder's book, *The Value of Your Soul* is just such a treasure. How fortunate that her journey can contribute so richly to our own."

—Philip Gulley, Quaker pastor, writer, and author of *Unlearning God: How Unbelieving Helped Me Believe, and numerous other works of nonfiction and fiction*

"This is an exceedingly charming volume, as beautiful as it is important. Snyder intertwines an original, obliquely angled re-vision of passages from Rumi's poetry and prose with an intriguing memoir into a resplendent tapestry. Both the thirteenth-century mystic and the twenty-first-century searcher bridge the personal to the universal in compelling ways."

—Ori Z. Soltes, professor of theology, philosophy, and art history at Georgetown University and author of *Mysticism in Judaism, Christianity, and Islam: Searching for Oneness*

"*Man plans*, the Yiddish adage goes, *and God laughs*. There is no shortage of surprises in life and some of those are crude tests of our ability to adapt, have self-control, and surrender. It is like an old friend consoling when she notes 'Sometimes you're given what you need, not what you think you want.' What gives power to these words is the very story of Snyder's day-to-day experiences at the Braemar retreat and how Rumi's lines help her navigate through the uncertain, unexpected, and yes, the annoying! Snyder's engaging style makes the book a pleasant read on the borderlines of our contemporary lives and Rumi's ecstatic orbit."

—Ibrahim Anli, executive director of the Rumi Forum, Washington, D.C.

"Poetry is said to be timeless. The poetry of the thirteenth-century Sufi mystic Mawlana Jalaladdin Rumi is some of the most beautiful ever written. Since its discovery by the West, it has transformed and moved countless individuals; S.A. Snyder is among them. In this wonderful book, she intricately weaves Rumi's poetry with her experience of living in Scotland at a spiritual retreat. Her book shows the continuing value of Rumi to our world today and is a must read for both those who have been reading Rumi for years and those new to the great Sufi poet."

—Zeki Saritopak, professor of Islamic studies in the Department of Theology and Religious Studies and the Bediüzzaman Said Nursi Chair in Islamic studies at John Carroll University; author of *Islam's Jesus*

The Value of Your Soul

Rumi Verse for Life's Annoying Moments

S.A. Snyder

First Edition

Print ISBN: 978-1-7332925-3-5

Cover and book design by Melissa Williams Design
Illustrations and cover art by Simon Blackwood

 Luna River
PUBLISHING, LLC

www.LunaRiverPublishing.com

When I read excerpts of the draft for this book to my mom, she said, "How did you get to be so wise?" Well, Mom, I was brung up good! So this book is for you, the woman who taught me all I know.

And to all seekers everywhere, especially those wanting relief from the silly things we humans get up to when we forget the value of our souls.

Listen if you
can bear listening [. . .]
[. . .] the words of knowers
are all about seeing

—Nader Khalili, translator, The Spiritual Poems of Rumi

Foreword

Jelal ad-Din Rumi was a thirteenth-century Sufi poet whose teachings could hardly resonate more powerfully in the world of the twenty-first century. A mystic, his teachings were devoted to connecting one's self to God: God as the Beloved, and the mystic as the lover—except that as the mystic seeks God, God seeks the mystic, so God is also the Lover and the mystic the beloved. Put otherwise, the mystic seeks to be filled with God. The mystic needs to be emptied of self—of ego—for that process to have a chance of succeeding.

This means at least three things: One, that while Rumi is an intense Muslim, he is simultaneously a universalist—it is our egos, informing the politics of religion, that cause us to imagine that "my faith is the only true form of faith." Rumi is particularly eloquent at recognizing and expressing the idea that in a world, all of which and everyone within which was created by God, with an infinite variety of leaves, snowflakes, and human beings—none identical—it would be absurd not to recognize an infinity of plausible paths to God.

Two, if God created us all, then to love God is to love all of creation—its trees and its chickens and geese, its chilling rain, and its diverse humanity.

Three, if my goal as a mystic is enlightenment for myself, then I won't succeed: that goal is too *selfish*; in divesting myself of ego, my goal must be to become enlightened enough to help improve the community around me.

These ideas are expressed repeatedly in Rumi's writings: "Every holy person seems to have a different doctrine and practice, but there's really only one work" is one of the many verses in which he makes this point.

How appropriate a messenger of wide-spread hope in a world that, particularly in the past several years, has become increasingly fractious and fractured. Ours is one among many countries in which the current, profoundly ego-bound leadership seeks to tear us apart, rather than bring us together. These are the ones who cannot bear to listen, who see only themselves. Those who read and hear the words of this volume, on the other hand, will be immeasurably enriched, both by the sage and passionate prose and poetic passages from Rumi, and by S.A. Snyder's original and wonderfully oblique translations of Rumi's thought into contemporary applicability through her own memoir of a compelling spiritual and intellectual pilgrimage.

Her experiences during her two-year-long journey within the billows of southeastern Scotland in the early twenty-first century weave themselves comfortably around those of Jelal ad-Din Rumi in central Turkey eight centuries ago. She does in her way what he does in his: apply a rich range of intense personal experience to a world of everyman and everywoman. Nothing could resonate more sonorously in a world fraught with viruses of varied forms.

—Ori Z. Soltes

Professor of theology, philosophy, and art history at Georgetown University and author of *Mysticism in Judaism, Christianity, and Islam: Searching for Oneness*

If you know the value of every article of merchandise, but you don't know the value of your own soul, it will all have been pointless.

—Kabir Helminski, translator, *The Pocket Rumi*

Introduction

When my friend Jill died after a twenty-five-year battle with breast cancer, I inherited her books of Rumi poetry. I had been introduced to Rumi several years before meeting Jill, and she and I shared our love for the thirteenth-century Islamic scholar and Sufi mystic. Sufism is an order of the Muslim faith, and its practioners are sometimes called whirling dervishes for the moving meditation they practice, which involves ritualistic spinning in circles. The meditation is a graceful dance, the purpose of which is to remember our human origins as coming from God. Rumi was, and still is, widely adored for his brilliant love poems to God. While thumbing through Jill's books after her death, I would come across a bookmark here, a scrap of paper there, or a sticky tab affixed to a page. I read the poems on those pages to get a sense of what she might have been experiencing at the time she bookmarked them.

Jill and I often confided in each other the things we

found annoying about life, other people, and our struggles in trying to lead a spirit-centered existence. We shared many of the same beliefs and experiences; we shared a love of nature and the arts, as well as a similar sense of humor. We also had our differences. There were things that significantly annoyed her but which seemed trivial to me. Such is human nature: what matters to one matters little to another. Nevertheless, Jill was a great sounding board for me because she got me.

Jill and I met when she was in her late fifties and me in my mid-thirties. She was an Englishwoman, I an American. We were both women of faith—she a Quaker, I a lapsed Christian—yet our hearts had been longing to connect with a deeper way of living. We both ached with an abiding desire for a more profound connection to the Divine. Our individual journeys on the path of spiritual enrichment coincided at a retreat center called Braemar (not its real name) in Scotland. Our friendship spanned the last seven years of her life.

Built in 1752, Braemar House was a minor manor home with surrounding estate lands in the wildland moors of the Scottish Borders. I don't know the expanse of the original estate, but when I lived there in the late 1990s it occupied just under two hundred acres amid a broader landscape of rolling green pastures, scattered spruce plantations, and hardscrabble sheep farms. The Braemar estate comprised grassland hillsides, woodlands, ponds, a partially-walled vegetable garden, and a few acres of landscaped grounds. A couple of cottages housed some of the residents, while a big stone barn converted into a dormitory housed adult students who came to pursue a deeper relationship and understanding of God.

At the time Jill and I lived at Braemar, the retreat center primarily hosted the Six Month Course, to which adult students from all over the world applied themselves in what Braemar referred to as "esoteric studies." Jill was one of the students. At its heart were the inspired writings of a twelfth-century Muslim scholar, Sufi mystic, and philosopher called Ibn Arabi. His and Rumi's lives intersected as Islamic philosophers. Ibn Arabi wrote about the nature of God, the human relationship with God, and humankind's place in the universe. The students, from all types of backgrounds and religious beliefs, studied Ibn Arabi, Rumi, and other philosophical and spiritual writings through a rigorous schedule of work, study, and meditation. Volunteer staff taught the courses and maintained the communal household. Students and staff all pitched in, living together, sharing meals, and doing their assigned work to keep the place running. On average, around twenty to forty people lived at Braemar at any given time. Numbers would drop when there wasn't a course being taught and swell during certain holidays with visitors, including global "Braemarites" (those who had taken courses and were spiritually invested in the teachings) and others who discovered Braemar through word of mouth or, like me, stumbled across it on the internet.

I was in crisis at the time, which is usually how these types of stories begin. At age thirty-four, my life in Montana felt like a dead-end. My job was not a career but something I did to pay the bills and get health insurance. Most of my friends had moved away, and I had no romantic prospects. I was bored and lonely and resentful that my life wasn't turning out the way I had envisioned. I started searching the internet for something different, with a strong desire to leave the country. I picked the United Kingdom because I had previously spent a lot of time there and felt a strong connection to my ancestral roots.

Through a series of connections, I learned about a tree planting project at some place called Braemar. The backstory, which I didn't know until after I arrived, was that the Scottish government was handing out grants to private landowners and conservation-minded nonprofits to reforest their properties with native trees. Braemar had received one of these grants from the Millennium Forest for Scotland Trust to plant seventeen thousand trees on about ten hectares of their large estate. The trees would replace former spruce plantations that had been logged in the 1980s. Braemar invited me to participate. The fit was perfect, given my university degree in forestry. This is how I became volunteer staff, only I soon learned there was a lot more to my role. In addition to forestry, I found myself taking care of livestock, working in the garden, and performing every manner of chore required for the upkeep of the two-hundred-acre property. And when I say "I found myself," I mean that also in the philosophical sense because I had rediscovered the essence of my soul. I found my *Self.* It was the best of times and worst of times.

While I was putting together this collection of stories, it occurred that they all fell within categories representing some of the most powerful human emotions: fear, resentment, disappointment, isolation, vulnerability, impatience, expectation, and control. To experience them guarantees plenty of annoying moments in life. We humans are especially good at blaming others for what ails us without considering that we are the agents of our own making. Some of us choose to learn life's lessons the hard way, while others make it look easy, and still others seem never to learn at all. There is probably a little of each in everyone: Some lessons must be repeated over and over, while others we learn quickly. Some lessons we never get, forcing us into an endless state of lifelong—and unnecessary—annoyance.

Whenever I need an emotional pick-me-up (or a stop-your-griping kick in the backside), I turn to Rumi. His words make me forget the trivial things I so tightly grasp and remind me of life's true essence—Spirit. One of my favorite lines in all of Rumi's poetry is this: *When the soul lies down in that grass, the world is too full to talk about.* Have you ever lied down in the grass and gazed at the sky or the branches of a tree? Nothing else matters in those moments, not with all the endless beauty that surrounds us, from the minutia of a tiny insect to the vastness of the sky and beyond. This simple act of taking time out, by itself, can heal the soul.

The personal experiences I share in this book taught me a few important lessons for better living. They are captured from my two years living at Braemar, and you can find the full stories and more in my memoir, *Plant Trees, Carry Sheep.* Think of this book as lamb stew for the annoyed soul, or memoir lite. Though these stories deal with unpleasant human emotions and practices, they are also about love, forgiveness, and letting go. My intent is to make you feel less isolated or less bad about yourself while also asking you to consider reflective questions and suggestions for soothing annoying circumstances. These "negative" emotions are natural and they teach us about compassion for others as well as for ourselves. At the very least, I hope you can enjoy a chuckle and forget about your troubles for a while.

Sometimes I wonder what my friend Jill would make of all the seemingly senseless and irrational events that have happened in the world since her death in 2005. What poems would she bookmark today to help her cope? I have left the paper scraps and sticky tabs in her books of Rumi poetry. There's a sacredness to keeping those pages marked, like hanging onto an article of clothing that a long-gone loved one once wore. Jill definitely wore Rumi's poetry. Maybe one day while I'm re-reading those marked pages, she'll speak to me, whisper a timely message in my ear, or simply proclaim, *I'm here and I am listening.*

My wish for you is that in reading these stories you too feel that someone is listening; someone who understands what you're going through, the little ways you chastise yourself or make life more difficult than it needs to be. You deserve relief from suffering. Have a lie-down in that grass awhile and take in the surrounding beauty. Contemplate the value of your soul; it is priceless beyond any human measure. You are more than the sum of that which annoys you. You are human, and that's just Divine!

About the Rumi Translations

When selecting the verses to accompany each "annoyance," I marked the ones I thought might fit somewhere. But when I went back to assign each to a chapter, there were a few I couldn't understand why I had marked. The meaning either became obscure on second reading or it didn't seem to fit after all. In some cases I found another poem and in other cases, I stuck with the original until its meaning unfolded to me. Such is the nature of poetry. What may resonate one day may not another because we are different from day to day. We are literally and figuratively fluid; not only do our cells continuously change, and fluids continuously flow through our bodies, so do our minds, our emotions, and thoughts continuously change.

In some cases I have slightly modified the translations of Rumi to be more contemporary (for example, changing "man" to "person" and using the gender-neutral "they" instead of "he"). The goal here is not to remain true to the precise wording; even the translators have taken liberties from the original Farsi. Some might have a problem with that, but I believe poetry is given to us. Its meaning is for the reader alone to decide. Poetry speaks to every individual differently, regardless of the poet's original intention. My goal, therefore, is to introduce new readers to Rumi or reconnect those already familiar with him. You may find different meaning in the selected verses, and if you do, I hope it helps!

I invite your soul to revel in more of Rumi's inspired works. See the bibliography for a list of books that contain the quoted material in this volume.

Note

This book does not address issues of abuse. So when I talk about surrender and acceptance, letting go of control, and other similar behaviors, it does not include accepting abuse. If you are in an abusive situation, please seek help even if you are uncertain whether your situation constitutes abuse. Call the National Domestic Violence Hotline at 1-800-799-7233. If you are unable to speak safely on the phone, visit www.thehotline.org or text LOVEIS to 1-866-331-9474.

Expectation Control

Yesterday I was clever, so I
wanted to change the world.

Today I am wise,
so I am changing myself.

Chapter 1

Annoyance

When you volunteer to plant trees but end up mucking out chicken coops.

Translation

Plans change.

Rumi Verse[1]

Inside each of us there's a continual autumn. Our leaves fall and are blown out over the water. [. . .] Very little grows on jagged rock. Be ground. Be crumbled, so wildflowers will come up where you are. You've been stony for too many years. Try something different. Surrender.

Unpacking It

When my desperately bored-with-life soul first reached out to Braemar from my home in Montana to offer my services in exchange for room and board, they invited me to come plant trees (see the Introduction). My initial contact was through a man named William, the manager of the estate grounds. What I didn't know was that eleven thousand trees had already been planted that previous April. Braemar intended to plant the remaining six thousand trees the following April. So when I arrived in September ready to plant trees, William told me the project was another six months away.

"What am I supposed to do in the meantime?" I asked him.

The response was something along the lines of, "Oh, there's plenty. You can bake bread, chop firewood, clean toilets, or do whatever needs doing. That's how it works here."

At that same time I also learned that William would soon be returning home to Australia, so Braemar would have a new estate manager. The new guy, Trevor, would be sort of like my boss, since he was going to be in charge of all the grounds-keeping and forestry work. Apparently,

---

1 Barks, Soul of Rumi, 21.

they had assumed I would take the role of the Trevor's assistant. It took me a few minutes to recover from the initial shock of this news, after which I learned what the role would entail. Braemar had small livestock to look after, firewood to harvest, a vegetable garden to revive from the dead, fences to mend, and all manner of miscellaneous "whatever needs doing." The position didn't excuse me from any potential toilet cleaning, however, because Braemar was truly a pitch-in place, although staff members—all volunteers—mostly stuck to their assigned roles. The toilet-cleaning of animals, though, was front and center.

I could have chosen to leave—and return home with my tail between my legs after having announced to God and country that I was moving to Scotland and not to be surprised if I ended up there for the rest of my life. Or I could stay and muck out chicken coops. I chose the muck. To my surprise, that choice transformed my life in ways I never dreamed (although not without first subjecting me to a lot of personal turmoil). I tried something different. I surrendered.

Ooh, *surrender*! That word used to stick in my craw because I interpreted it as giving up or giving in. However, I'm slowly making peace with surrender, which I now see more as giving up trying to control situations. It's also about accepting new opportunities when they present themselves because sometimes plans change. Typically, most people aren't fans of change. We like knowing what to expect. We find comfort in routine and certainty. Even if we don't like the routine we're stuck in, at least it's familiar. We don't like being taken off guard because we don't like surprises, unless it's a lottery win. If change and the unexpected scare you, buckle up because the only certain thing in life is change. One day we're going to our favorite restaurant or visiting friends or vacationing on the beach, and the next we're on global lockdown because of a deadly pandemic.

Try looking at it this way: Sometimes you're given what you need, not what you think you want. Change can improve your life or situation, lead to better health, deeper relationships, even fun! I reluctantly accepted my altered invitation at Braemar and in doing so learned a lot about myself, others, the world, and my place in it. I had to wade through lots of crap, chicken and otherwise, and that was entirely the point. It got me to a better place in myself. I learned to surrender to opportunities, even if they weren't part of the plan. I learned to accept that change happens, and how I respond to it makes all the difference to the outcome. Acceptance uses a lot less emotional energy and often results in much grander outcomes than I had imagined—even if it's a series of smaller changes that ultimately lead to something larger.

Rumi talks about the continual autumn in us, our fallen leaves blown out across the water. In other words, life is constantly changing; something is always dying away to make room for the new. Without change, we can't have spring wildflowers or new forests. Being willing to be fertile ground means being open to change. You never know, it could lead to amazing transformation.

Chapter 2

Annoyance

When moles make mounds on your perfect lawn.

Translation

You worry about little things that probably don't matter in the grander scheme, or you're not respecting other people's preferences.

Rumi Verse[2]

We're quite addicted to subtle discussions; we're very fond of solving problems. So that we may tie knots and then undo them, we constantly make rules for posing the difficulty and for answering the questions it raises. We're like a bird which loosens a snare and then ties it tighter again in order to perfect its skill. It deprives itself of open country; it leaves behind the meadowland, while its life is spent dealing with knots. Even then the snare is not mastered, but its wings are broken again and again. Don't struggle with knots, so your wings won't be broken. Don't risk ruining your feathers to display your proud efforts.

Unpacking It

There were two of us on the Braemar estate team, and one of us cared *way* more than the other about an alleged mole "problem." The problem consisted of a few resident moles and their unobtrusive dirt hills on an otherwise croquet-perfect lawn, complete with diagonal stripes. Had Braemar been a genteel British manor with a huge budget to employ staff who were solely dedicated to landscaping, we might not have had the mole problem. However, Braemar was more impoverished than genteel, so we had to settle for two full-time volunteers (me and the other person who cared way too much about mole hills) to manage two hundred acres that included a one-acre vegetable garden and livestock. Needless to say, we were fond of plant life that took care of itself.

The new estate manager, Trevor, tried many tactics

---

2 Helminksi and Helminski, Rumi Daylight, 204

to catch (traps), eradicate (mole bombs), and intimidate (water hose down the hole) the moles. With great fervor, he would shovel up their mounds into a wheelbarrow and dump the fine soil in the garden. The next day, more mounds would pop up like, well, like the beloved carnival game Whac-A-Mole. The mole mounds, which I regarded as a trivial matter, annoyed Trevor to no end. His obsession annoyed me because I felt he should live and let live. At one point he succeeded at moving the mole community along, but in my opinion it cost a lot of needless time and effort. And the moles eventually came back anyway.

Did mole mounds on the lawn matter? We could have found a way to coexist with a few of the little creatures. Maybe Trevor was overly concerned. And maybe I could have accepted his preference for a mole-free lawn. Probably we both could have met in the middle.

We all have our pet peeves and we all know people who are bothered by things that seem inconsequential to us. Is it our place to tell them their pet peeves are trivial? Trevor was determined to create an estate worthy of being featured in a coffee-table book. For some reason, having a picture-perfect lawn brought him great pleasure. Who was I to tell him otherwise? Suffice to say we drove each other batty with our differing preferences and peeves. In retrospect, we could have discussed our steadfast individual quirks and reasons for them to gain insight about each other, potentially creating more empathy between us.

You aren't required to understand others' quirks, but you can attempt to accept them and let slide the harmless ones. You can also examine your own quirks with an eye toward lightening up and refraining from imposing yourself on others. Rumi talks about tying ourselves into knots. In what ways are you tying yourself in knots to perfect something of little value? Or maybe you gripe about things you have no control over and which are best left alone. There is a certain freedom in loosening a snare and flying free as opposed to trying to master the snare, which may only just trap you again and again. Whether it's your snare of perfection or another's, sometimes it's best to just walk away.

Chapter 3

Annoyance

When the tractor gets stuck in the mud.

Translation

The way forward gets you nowhere even faster, or difficulties hound you.

Rumi Verse[3]

Learn the alchemy that enlightened ones know: the moment you accept what troubles you have been given, the door will open. Welcome difficulty as a familiar comrade. Joke with torment brought by the Friend.

Unpacking It

By far the most used piece of equipment on the Braemar estate, after the fencing pliers and broad axe, was the FiatAgri tractor with bucket and forklift. We drove it everywhere, towing a huge green trailer that we could raise hydraulically to dump its contents (firewood and dirt mostly). Trevor made me learn how to drive the tractor during my first week on the job. By myself. While I sat in the seat, he showed me all the gears and controls. Then he sent me on my way, saying he'd meet me "on the other side." I assumed he meant around the bend and over the hill at one of the sections of the estate and not, you know, The Other Side. My assumption turned out to be correct, although for a long couple of minutes it was touch and go as I headed down a *really* steep hill on my maiden voyage along the gravel track that cut through part of the estate. The fifteen-minute experience frightened the liver out of me.

I could barely reach the pedals in the tractor cab, even with the seat pulled all the way forward. Oftentimes I would place a piece of split wood against the seat back for something to lean on while I sat on the edge of the seat. We used the tractor for hauling everything and for transporting ourselves and tools from one end of the huge

---

3   Barks, The Glance, 65.

estate to another. I got pretty good at reversing the tractor with the trailer attached, even through narrow gates. Another thing Trevor and I both were really good at was getting the tractor stuck in the mud.

Despite that its tires were nearly as tall as me, and wide (unlike me), the tiniest patch of mud could trap the one-ton vehicle like a fly on sticky paper. We'd set off eager to tackle the morning's work, and then splat, that was us stuck in the mud. We would spend the next couple of hours trying to unstick the tractor. Then we'd take a break for morning coffee and go back to the tractor forty minutes later. Then we'd take a break for lunch, and pretty soon there went the day with nary a task completed because of a little mud. Our unsticking method consisted mostly of gunning the engine and trying to roll the tractor back and forth in a low gear. It succeeded only in getting us more stuck. We were so determined to free it that we didn't think to leave it and go do something else instead. Eventually, we learned to drive around mud, even if it seemed harmless.

What could you do differently to ease some difficulty you're experiencing? Sometimes plunging ahead, obstacles be damned, isn't the best way forward. Stop and assess the risks. Go around if you have to, without trying to muscle through. Or, if you get stuck, relax. The mud will eventually dry up, and you can be on your way again. Rumi says to welcome our troubles like familiar friends—too familiar sometimes! The *Friend*, with a capital F, is God. I can't say whether God intentionally torments us, but I do know that life is full of mud holes that we allow to torment us. Laughing in the face of some of your difficulties might just give you the strength to make it through.

If you feel plagued by constant difficulty, what is this teaching you? My attitude about troubles has changed over the years from *Why does this always happen to me?*

to *What can I learn from this?* If disappointment strikes or the path forward is blocked, keep in mind that maybe there is something better in store on a different path. Once, I was forced to quit a high-paying job that I loved but then was offered an even better one later. Seeing my unemployment as a time to take stock rather than a difficulty helped me stay emotionally healthy. Sometimes constant difficulty is a sign that you might be better off finding another way around.

Chapter 4

When the wind blows your carefully raked leaf piles.

Translation

You're obsessed with what things look like, or you're putting in too much effort.

Rumi Verse[4]

Know that the outward form passes away, but the world of reality remains forever. How long will you play at loving the shape of the jug? Leave the jug; go, seek the water!

Unpacking It

Around the Braemar House grounds grew a small grove of mature oak, ash, and beech. As trees are wont to do, they dropped leaves in autumn. We were ankle deep in an acre of foliage, which Trevor wanted to gather and create what's called a leaf mold, which is a fancy British way of saying a big pile of leaves that eventually rots down to become lovely compost for the garden. What better way to collect a literal ton of leaves than with a leaf vacuum attached to our Iseki riding lawn mower? Only we didn't have a vacuum attachment nor could we afford to buy one, nor did we have a leaf blower because the noise of one would have been obnoxious at a retreat. So we did what all penny-pinching nonprofits would do: cleaned up the leaves the old-fashioned way.

We raked and raked and raked. A couple of guests dropped in during that time, and we made them rake. At the end of two back-breaking, arm-cramping, hand-blistering weeks, we had gathered dozens of tidy leaf piles around the grounds. The trees had nearly finished shedding, so we made plans to gather the piles and move them to form a small mountain outside the chicken field—the leaf mold. It would take a couple of days to move the individual piles of leaves, wheelbarrow load by wheelbarrow load, to the leaf mold. We went to bed content in

---

4   Helminksi and Helminski, Rumi Daylight, 124.

the knowledge that we'd soon be done with this labor-intensive project. That night a gale-force wind thundered across the moors. It was the type of wind that rattled windows and doors, kept people awake, and made everyone look like zombies the next morning at the breakfast table. Guess what happened to two weeks' worth of carefully raked leaf piles?

Rumi tells us to stop loving the shape of the jug, the container, and instead focus on what the container holds. In other words, stop obsessing about what things look like and seek the true essence of life. He was speaking about our physical selves and encouraging us to seek what it means to be made of the Spirit that we are. However, we can apply this concept to just about anything (see chapters 2 and 11). In the case of the Great Leaf Debacle we were obsessed with making the house grounds look tidy by clearing them of nature's litter. Heaven forfend leaves should be on the ground beneath a canopy of trees! I guess Spirit was teaching us a lesson: *You don't like my leaves? Poof!* We did re-rake them, only the second time we filled wheelbarrows full and moved them to the mold as we went along. We also weren't as obsessed with getting every single leaf.

Are you obsessed with appearances, such as a leaf-free lawn or your body, perhaps? We all want to look our best or create the best-looking thing—whatever that is—but proceed with caution. Are you obsessing about perfection for perfection's sake or is the juice worth the squeeze? Our fondness for perfection sometimes leads to useless effort (raking an acre of leaves by hand, for instance). Instead, try equipping yourself with the right metaphorical or literal tools—a different way of thinking or leaf vacuum, for instance. Don't let perfect be the enemy of good enough.

Chapter 5

Annoyance

When your sheep escape constantly.

Translation

Things—and people—you are trying to control are not behaving the way you want them to.

Rumi Verse[5]

When one sheep of the flock jumps over a stream, they all jump across on each other's heels. Drive the sheep, your senses, to pasture. Let them feed on the pasture shown by He who has brought forth the herbage that they may graze on hyacinth and wild rose; and be led to the green meadows of the Realities; that every one of their senses may become a prophet to the others, and lead all senses into that paradise.

Unpacking It

For several months we kept a band of seven sheep ewes of a variety called Soay. Soays are a rare breed named after a Scottish Hebridean island on which they used to run wild many centuries ago. "Rare breed" in this case, however, means not that their species is dwindling but rather that people *rarely* want to own Soays because they're such a PITA (pain in the behind). Soays are semi-wild. They have a mind of their own and pretty much do whatever they want. They're also difficult to confine, and even blue-ribbon sheep dogs have a hard time herding them. Our Soay field had inadequate fencing, and we didn't have the money to improve it. So we used various bits and bobs to patch the holes and weak spots—barbed wire, old boards from the barn, leftover breakfast porridge. Yet no matter how many times we patched and plugged, the sheep found their way through the fence. They also began making new holes in the chicken wire at the bottom or dug under it and crawled out. Alcatraz would not have contained the little devils.

---

5 Helminksi and Helminski, Rumi Daylight, 182.

The sheep were after the luscious tall grass in the field next to theirs, which also happened to include a budding orchard of sapling trees. Sheep love succulent young tree leaves almost as much as they love grass. Sheep in tree field = guaranteed death of saplings. Sometimes they also went for a romp in the neighboring farmer's field. He was not pleased. We were forever patching holes and chasing the sheep back to our field. In other words, we were trying to control a situation: a) without properly addressing the root of the issue—poor fencing; and b) that ultimately was going to do what it wanted to do anyway.

Control. For some the thought of control brings a mouth-watering pleasure; for others, a bad aftertaste or maybe a skin-crawling aversion. Admit it, though, even if you have no desire to wield control over others even some-times (*you* are a rare breed, by the way), who doesn't want control over their own life? You may be confusing control of yourself with control of others or a situation. If you learn only one thing in life, let it be this: The only things you have control over are your behaviors and responses. You CANNOT *fully* control other living things or situa-tions. You can *influence* by various means, but ultimately, all able-minded adults have full agency over themselves, and results are mostly governed by their choices. Have you noticed that sometimes no matter how much you try to control situations, they just don't turn out the way you want, having nothing to do with you or your actions?

You can safely let go of your need to control while still maintaining your responsibility to guide and influence others entrusted to you: minors, the incapacitated, sheep. Regarding our Soays, we controlled whether we spent money for adequate fencing or chose not to get sheep in the first place. We couldn't control typical Soay behavior of strong independence and a complete lack of respect for the fence boundaries. So with that in mind, we decided to

let them graze the grass in the tree field, which was chok-
ing out the saplings anyway. Guess what? Every night
the sheep returned to their rightful field. No chasing, no
aggravation, no swearing. In the meantime, we worked
on upgrading the fence. Eventually, it became clear that
we had only so much influence and resources to keep the
Soays contained, so we sold them. (Please don't try this
with your children.)

Let go of control and find other ways to manage what
you have, leaving the stress behind. Or find peaceful ways
to coexist with the people and things that cause you distress. Or don't get involved in the first place, if possible.
Control the unruly sheep of your own tendencies first and
graze in the green meadows of what is real, what truly
matters in life. Then lead others by example.

Chapter 6

Annoyance

When only some of your eggs hatch.

Translation

You bank on something that might not happen and then it bothers you when it doesn't, even though you knew better.

Rumi Verse[6]

To practice patience is the soul of praise: have patience, for that is true glorification. No glorification is worth as much. Have patience: patience is the remedy for pain.

Unpacking It

One spring we decided to collect and hatch ourselves the eggs of our poultry flocks: chickens, turkeys, ducks, and geese. We started with seven goose eggs, which I put in an incubator meant only for a dozen chicken eggs. The goose eggs barely fit. The incubator was designed to gently turn the eggs every twelve hours, but the large goose eggs got the mechanism off balance. This meant *I* had to turn them by hand every twelve hours. Also, I was supposed to mist the eggs with water, "not too warm, not too cool," said the instructions (not too helpful). Goose eggs take an average of thirty days to hatch, so I kept up this ritual for thirty-seven days before giving up. Consumed with the guilt of waste, and annoyed that it didn't work, I threw the eggs out. Would the geese have more successfully hatched them? Sort of. Later they managed to hatch one gosling from a clutch of eight eggs.

We tried forty chicken eggs in a much larger incubator. We had big dreams of tripling our flock, securing tons more eggs, and eating the extra cockerels. With the upgraded incubator, all I had to do was mist the eggs every once in a while to ensure they got the right amount of moisture. When the hatching day arrived, I was awakened by a little peeping at 5 AM. My first chick! I watched, mesmerized, through the window in the incubator lid as the other eggs began to emerge. Eventually, only eleven of

---

6   Helminksi and Helminski, Rumi Daylight, 178.

the forty eggs produced a chick. Of those, nine survived. At this rate it would take several batches to double our flock. We tried incubating a few more batches. In the end only fifteen chicken chicks grew into adults. Most of them were males, which didn't advance our plans for increased egg production. The duck eggs didn't fare much better and presented us with different problems (see Chapter 32). We were sorely disappointed, especially because of all the effort we put into incubating 120 eggs. Paltry—not *poultry*—returns on our investment.

Sometimes things just don't work out as planned, and that's not always a bad thing. We hadn't thought about the care needed to tend to the chicks, had all the eggs hatched. For starters, we'd have had to build more coops. As it stood, raising fifteen chicks was a lot of work. We had daily feeding and cleaning of their quarters, and we had to graduate them from different size enclosures as they grew to protect them from predators until they were big enough to survive in the flock. We could have let the birds hatch their own eggs, although with the predator problem, any hatched chicks probably wouldn't have lived long without intervention anyway. Our fourth attempt produced equally low returns, then gradually our success increased. To be honest, we had no clue what we were doing at first, so you could say that our initial *eggspectations* were out of sync with reality. With trial and error—and lots of patience—we got better. We decided to treat incubating eggs as more of a hobby than a game changer, which also helped.

What are you counting on perhaps unrealistically? How will you respond if it doesn't turn out the way you planned? Don't bank on what you don't have nor are guaranteed. If the loss would be catastrophic, consider alternative options. Sometimes not getting what you hope for is a blessing in camouflage. On the other hand, patience can bring not only rewards, it can be a balm for expectation.

Chapter 7

Annoyance

When the power goes out during inconvenient moments.

Translation

We expect everything to always work out the way it's supposed to.

Rumi Verse[7]

Rumi tells a story about an eagle that swoops down and takes Mohammad's boot just as he was about to put it on. Mohammad grows angry that the eagle has flown off with his boot. But then the eagle dumps out a poisonous snake that was in the boot. When Mohammad saw this, he was grateful and thanked the eagle, who returned the boot. Rumi continues: *When misfortune comes, you must quickly praise. Others may be saying oh no, but you will be opening out like a rose losing itself petal by petal. [. . .] Don't grieve for what doesn't come. Some things that don't happen keep disasters from happening.*

Unpacking It

Braemar was off the grid and our electricity came from two temperamental diesel-powered generators, affectionately known as the big jenny and the little jenny. We also called them not-so-affectionate things when they stopped working, plunging us into darkness or another state of powerless inconvenience. The little jenny was used for times of low-power demand, usually after 10 PM through to breakfast or so. Braemar's maintenance man, Rafi, turned the big jenny on when demand for power was high. This was typically in the evening when lights were needed or when we had lots of guests, or when we used energy-sucking appliances such as the old-fashioned ironing press. (Beautifully pressed linen tablecloths at every meal belied our humble existence as penniless seekers of God.)

Rafi was forever doing battle with the jennys, which

---

7 Barks, *Essential Rumi*, 170-1.

frequently crashed for no apparent reason. We couldn't afford new generators nor afford to hook up to the main power grid. Thankfully, Rafi was a crack mechanic, who always managed to get the jennys turned back on. Who knows how much worse off we would have been if it hadn't been for his skills at tweaking, cursing, and throwing his wrench across the generator shed? As if to pacify these machines, he even painted the inside of the shed a bright white color. Of course, that could have been to improve his own environment, seeing as how he spent many hours in that generator shed.

Needless to say, appliances such as hair dryers, electric space heaters, and electric kettles were banned because they drew too much power. Rafi constantly reminded us of this fact and was convinced that one or another forbidden appliance was hidden somewhere in every room (his suspicions weren't entirely false). He frequently lectured us at mealtimes, scanned rooms during garbage collection day (he went room to room collecting trash), or chased us down in the dorm hallways as we tried to escape unnoticed, contraband hair dryer in hand.

Most times the jenny failures weren't so bad, but because some of the radiators relied on electricity to regulate the flow of hot water, it could get quite cold while waiting for Rafi to work his magic. Or the students' work would be interrupted because they couldn't see to scrub whatever it was they were scrubbing or chop whatever it was they were chopping during meal preparation. The worst was when you were writing a document on the computer and hadn't pressed the SAVE button in a while. Sometimes the jennys crashed while we were watching television and always happened right when the detective was about to confront the killer, or the next victim was about to be attacked, or the lovers were about to have hot sex.

We take for granted that most things in the world

usually work properly more often than not. Lights turn on when we need them, water flows from the tap (although see Chapter 33), and computers do what we want them to (that was a joke). Braemar's faltering electricity was annoying but never life-threatening—at least as far as we knew. The place was full of so many prehistoric appliances with outdated power cords that maybe Divine Providence swooped in to stop the flow of electricity before an odd spark could set the place on fire. We'll never know.

If everything worked out perfectly all the time, how would we learn to cope with the inevitable pitfalls of life? Technically, if everything worked out perfectly all the time, we'd have no pitfalls; however, that's unlikely. You may know people whom you believe to be charmed because everything always works out perfectly for them. But I bet they make life look easy because of their *attitude* toward it, not because everything really *is* easy.

Whether the electricity goes out, the car breaks down, or an eagle makes off with your boot, there may be a good reason behind it. So rather than curse inconvenience, be like a rose opening up in praise for what *is* given. Petals will eventually drop off—that is inevitable—yet new roses bloom in their wake.

Chapter 8

Annoyance

When your too-big garden is full of beans, leeks, cabbage, and potatoes, as well as weeds and slugs.

Translation

You're trying to do too much.

Rumi Verse[8]

How should spring bring forth a garden on hard stone? Become earth, that you may grow flowers of many colors. For you have been a heart-breaking rock. Once, for the sake of experiment, be earth!

Unpacking It

Braemar had a half-acre Victorian-era walled garden. Three sides of the wall had long since crumbled, but one could imagine what it once looked like. There were eight planting beds, each about fifty feet by thirty feet, which were divided down the middle with a twelve-foot-high beech hedge, complete with a shaped arch passageway. There was also a small greenhouse on one end where we started seeds in winter to plant out in early spring.

The estate manager, Trevor, was an idealist and he liked to experiment. His approach to work was to blast them with all you got and see what sticks. I was a realist, a planner always thinking about the consequences of everything we did. Experimenting was fine as long as we could manage the results. Not surprisingly, we disagreed on the best way to do pretty much everything. And because a half acre of growing space wasn't enough, Trevor decided we needed a separate quarter-acre potato field and three polytunnels—hoop houses—which are basically small Quonset huts covered in heavy-duty plastic. Our growing space more than doubled.

You could stick just about any seed in the ground at Braemar and it would sprout, especially given the mounds of horse poo and compost we worked into the soil (see Chapter 31). So Trevor's experiment paid off in

---

8 Helminksi and Helminski, Rumi Daylight, 51.

spades from a growing perspective, much to the delight of the wood pigeons, slugs, and the occasional neighbor's escaped lambs, all of which believed the bounty was meant for them. On the one hand, I was happy for Trevor and impressed with his success at growing anything. The parsnips were the size of his forearm, and the cabbages as big as soccer balls! On the other hand, his plan created additional weeding, hoeing, and pest control responsibilities— time-consuming tasks among multitudes of tasks needing attention on the estate. To give the garden due care, we would need five full-time gardeners.

In the broader scheme, the flourishing garden was a great achievement, although at the height of the harvest season, there weren't enough people living at Braemar to eat all of its bounty. Much of it was turned back into compost. I tried distancing myself from garden affairs to focus on things that didn't seem to overwhelm me so much. Every time I entered the garden, I felt paralyzed by all the upkeep. Eventually, I learned to take a page out of Trevor's seed catalog. I learned to be earth and let things grow as they needed, enjoying the beauty and bounty and letting go of the obsession to perfectly manage it all.

Have you planted too many things in your garden? Could you handle all the fruits of your labor if they did produce? Know your limits and have a plan for all conceivable outcomes, including if none of it turns out the way you expected. Try doing a few things well first before attempting to feed the world. Alternatively, let some things go without feeling the need to manage and control.

Chapter 9

Annoyance

When you think you're flying a Cessna but it turns out to be a microlight.

Translation

You have unspoken expectations or have trouble living in the moment.

Rumi Verse[9]

No need to announce the future! This now is it.
This. Your deepest need and desire is satisfied by
the moment's energy here in your hand.

Unpacking It

Braemar's maintenance man, Rafi, had a pilot's license to fly small aircraft. He had built his own kit plane, which he had flown to Braemar and kept tied down in a field. One day a gale-force wind knocked some pieces off and the plane was grounded in a shed. When he left Braemar, two years later, Rafi carted the pieces away on a trailer.

Nevertheless, Rafi wanted to keep his pilot's license current, which meant logging some flight time. He invited me and two others, Trevor and Shane, to go flying. For some reason, we jumped at the chance to be his test passengers. We packed ourselves into Rafi's Volvo station wagon and drove up north to a little airport outside Edinburgh. Shane was a fellow staff resident who helped in the kitchen and was a good friend of mine and Trevor's. He was unkempt, sometimes crude, and as lovable as he was annoying. A bout of meningitis in his twenties had left him with a child-like simplicity yet he also had a surprising depth of wisdom.

My dad had a license to fly small aircraft, and as a teenager I had flown with him several times in a four-seater Cessna. I used to love those joyrides and the sweeping views of the Midwestern suburbs and surrounding farmland where we lived. Now I had the chance to see the Scottish landscape from above. When we pulled into the airport, all we saw were microlights, best described

---

9   Helminksi and Helminski, *Rumi Daylight*, 51.

as two-seater motorcycles attached to a hang glider. Watching one of these contraptions buzz down the runway to get airborne tempts you to pray for the two souls sitting astride it. If the Flintstones had airplanes, this is what they would look like.

"We're going in one of *them?*" Shane asked, as we drove toward the parking lot in a grassy field.

Rafi said something to the effect of "yeah, what did you think?"

Although okay with enclosed small aircraft, I have a disabling fear of open-air heights. Riding a flying motorcycle wouldn't help my cause. Even Trevor, who had once gone skydiving, thereby demonstrating more of a daredevil spirit than Shane and me, was stunned into silence. Rafi parked the car and hopped out, eager to start flying. The rest of us sat motionless. Rafi was clearly annoyed.

"Oh come on, you lot! We came all the way out here to fly. You can't back out now!" he shouted through the driver's side door, which he hadn't shut yet.

Slowly, we three opened our doors and stepped out of the car with all the enthusiasm of arriving at the dentist's for a root canal.

In the airfield office, we signed the required forms absolving our families of the right to sue if we were killed. Rafi could only take us in the air one at a time, so we drew straws to see who would go first. Shane drew the short straw. We had to help dress him in the heavily-padded flight suit, he was that terrified. He had said nothing but a few words since getting out of the car, which was highly uncharacteristic for him. Standing by the flying machine, we patted Shane on the shoulder and told him it had been nice knowing him. He put on his helmet and saluted us, not a proper military salute but the kind you give a fellow driver who cuts you off in traffic.

Have you ever gone into something expecting one

thing and getting another? I thought so! In fact, I bet you've experienced numerous unmet expectations since the day you emerged from the comfort of a warm, dark womb into the cold, glaring lights of the delivery room; since the day you first went off to kindergarten expecting your classmates to love you as much as your parents did and your teacher to spoil you as much as your grandparents did. School would be endless years of fun and play! How did *that* work out for you?

It's called expectation and it gets us into trouble every time. Despite that expectation is the gateway to disappointment, we insist on having them and are surprised or upset when they aren't met. So if you have any, and you'd be really upset if they weren't met, speak up! The grander your expectations, the more you had better clarify them with all relevant parties, including yourself. Know what you're getting into, especially when you expect to fly high. Also, don't deliberately withhold information that would help others have reasonable expectations. That's just unfair and sneaky.

When Rafi and Shane landed forty-five minutes later, Shane couldn't stop talking. "I reckon that was the most brilliant thing I ever done in me life!" he said over and over in his Yorkshire accent.

Likewise, Trevor and I thoroughly enjoyed our flights. Which is another side to this lesson: You can leave your expectations in the parking lot and just go along. Be willing to experience whatever happens and see what happens. You might be delightfully surprised. Rumi knew the secret to life, that *this now is it*. Our deepest needs and desires can be fulfilled by the energy of the moment. Grab hold and fly, expectation free!

Resentment

Disappointment

Impatience

These pains you feel are messengers.
Listen to them.

Chapter 10

Annoyance

When your grain spills all over the road.

Translation

Sometimes skimping on money costs you more in the long run; or you fail to think a plan through logically and to account for the consequences.

Rumi Verse[10]

Rumi tells a story about a man who is transporting grain. He is loading two sacks on a camel when a nomad comes along and asks about them. The man tells the nomad one sack is full of grain and the other full of sand for balance. The nomad suggests that it might be wiser to fill each sack half full of the grain and forget the sand. Not only will the man not have to transport useless sand, but the load will be lighter for the camel. The man is so impressed with this advice that he offers to give the nomad a ride to his destination on his camel. Along the way, the man asks the nomad about his vocation. The nomad says he has nothing and lives nowhere; he relies instead on the kindness of strangers. Annoyed with the nomad, and disappointed that he's nothing but a lazy so-and-so, the man tells him to skedaddle, fearing that his bad luck will rub off on himself. Rumi continues: *Banish as a traveling companion the figuring, human intellect. Cunning rascals think the old ones know nothing because they're old. They dismiss patience and sacrifice and generosity, and the simplicity that does not calculate. That plain nomadic man opens a way for majesty, and majesty walks there.*

Unpacking It

Braemar raised turkeys, ducks, chickens, and geese. In total we cared for more than a hundred feathered creatures, which was a lot of mucking out of shelters, feeding,

---

10 Barks, Soul of Rumi, pg 147.

and watering. The chickens and turkeys got food scraps from the kitchen every morning, while the waterfowl foraged at the small lake outside the garden wall. We fed all of them supplemental barley, which meant we had to buy a half-ton load of feed grain every few months.

Always looking to save Braemar money, Trevor didn't want to pay the £25 delivery fee for the grain. So on our first—and only—trip to pick it up ourselves from the merchant, a half-hour drive away, we waited an hour for them to fill a gigantic nylon bag with the barley. They loaded the bulging bag onto our flatbed trailer, which we hauled with the Braemar Land Rover Defender, and weighed it. We paid our money and drove off. As we headed down the narrow country lanes back to Braemar, I glanced out the back window and noticed the bag was sagging to one side. I pointed this out to Trevor several times over the course of five winding miles. He ignored my suggestion to stop so that we could adjust the bag.

Several minutes later, I looked behind us again to see that the grain had started to flow out of the sagging bag. Without looking, Trevor said it was fine and told me to stop worrying. As he turned onto the main road, he glanced in the rearview mirror, swore, and hit the brakes. We scooped up what we could of the spilled barley and brushed about another fifteen pounds of it onto the road verge. After that incident, we paid to have the grain delivered.

In a related "cost-saving" measure, our poultry needed straw for their coops and pens, which a local farmer agreed to supply. Trevor insisted we retrieve the straw bales ourselves from the farmer's barn. The trouble was the straw was bundled into huge rolls and stacked five rolls high in the farmer's barn. We had to climb up a stack and push two of the bales down, sometimes from a height of fifteen feet.

After the bales were on the ground, we had to roll

them up onto the trailer, again towed by our workhorse Land Rover Defender. Keep in mind these bales weighed close to four hundred pounds. At best, all this effort was precarious; at worst, probably life endangering, not to mention time consuming. In the end, we realized it was more efficient to leave our trailer with the farmer so that he could load it with bales at his leisure using machinery appropriate for the job. We would then go back later to collect it.

If you're a cheapskate for cheapskate's sake ("I can do it for free! Why would I pay someone?"), think about this: What is your time worth? I've established an hourly rate for myself that I would expect to be paid to do a job. If a job I can do myself takes me more time or effort than I want to spend paying myself, I'll gladly hire someone instead. Doing so spreads the wealth in my community, and for some people that can mean the difference between making rent or not. On the other hand, if you truly can't afford to pay someone else, at least weigh your options and examine the consequences. Don't try to fix a complicated problem that is best left to the experts either for safety reasons or because if you mess it up, it will cost you more in the long run (plumbing and electricity come to mind). Heed the wise voice inside—or the advice of others in some cases (your spouse, for example). Just because someone doesn't appear to know the ways of the world, like Rumi's nomad dressed in rags, doesn't mean they can't give wise counsel. Avoid falling victim to the simplicity that does not calculate.

Chapter 11

Annoyance

When you clean the barn and someone dumps old shelving units in your tidy space.

Translation

Others keep messing up your little world.

Rumi Verse[11]

Out beyond ideas of wrongdoing and rightdoing, there is a field. I'll meet you there. When the soul lies down in that grass, the world is too full to talk about. Ideas, language, even the phrase "each other" doesn't make any sense.

Unpacking It

When I first arrived at Braemar I had grandiose plans for reviving the somewhat shabby grounds and gardens to a more respectable British country manor estate. While Trevor was obsessed with a mole-free lawn (see Chapter 2), I was obsessed with tidiness on a larger scale. The garden shed had been a dumping ground for tools, spare outdoor clothing, and chemicals; the area outside the garden wall became a dumping ground for rusted, nonfunctioning equipment, much of it unidentifiable. The old hay barn was used for storing anything that didn't fit in the garden shed, including broken furniture and used carpeting, as well as the proverbial and literal kitchen sink. Someone had salvaged the carpet from an old office building in England, thinking we might use it to re-carpet some of the dorm rooms (my room being one of them). Because the neighbor's sheep also had access to the hay barn, everything, including the carpet, was covered in poo.

Trevor and I spent a week clearing junk out of the hay barn, hauling it to the landfill, and neatly stacking and storing other useable items. We needed to make room for planks of wood that were starting to stack up in leaning heaps at the abandoned sawmill building because we wanted to free *that* space for other things. It was a musical

---

11   Moyne and Barks, Open Secret, Pg 8.

chairs game of storage. Not long after we finished tidying the hay barn, but before we could move the wood planks there, one of our fellow Braemarites noticed the freed-up space and promptly dumped—not stacked—a ton of salvaged steel shelving units that he got "for a really good deal." He even had the gall to thank us for clearing the space for him!

At Braemar it wasn't socially acceptable to physically harm people, so instead I shouted at him for being a selfish bonehead. He looked at me like an Irish wolfhound might look at a Chihuahua that was trying to scare it off with barking—half amused and half not understanding what all the fuss was about. I had behaved as if I owned the place and as if everyone should have known my intentions.

Sadly, this wasn't my first—or last—rodeo wherein I unilaterally decided what was and wasn't going to be the law. (In this case Trevor went along with my barn-clearing idea because I told him he couldn't have my help in the garden until the barn was cleared.) My insistence on having our outbuildings tidy and organized blinded me to the larger picture; that is, to what end this perfection? What does it matter, and why are no one else's objectives equally important? Further, let's all just forget about rules and go lie down in the grass, as Rumi muses, and take in more important things, like the beauty of life and how we're all connected.

Are you someone who expects others not only to abide by your "rules" but to also know what those rules are? You can't have everything *your* way, especially when you live with others. Try communicating your plans and compromising instead of viewing as inconvenience others messing up your world. Regarding that shelving, we were able to use most of it in the greenhouse, so it all worked out in the end.

Chapter 12

Annoyance

When you're forever mending fences.

Translation

You keep covering the same old ground over and over.

Rumi Verse[12]

I keep turning around this misfortune, this troubled illusion I call myself, when I could be turning around you, the giver of blessings, origin, and presence. [. . .] I turn around this frustrated body, tethered in a barn of words, when I could be free in the infinite pasture. Free, why do I keep turning as though fastened to a pole?

Unpacking It

Surrounded by sheep farms and subdivided into sections, our two hundred acres had miles upon miles of fencing. Most of it was in decent shape, but a lot of it was in crap shape—leaning posts, sagging wires, and gaps. Trevor once told me that in Scotland one had to fence the neighbors' livestock out rather than the neighbors having to fence their livestock in. Consequently, we were responsible for fixing the fencing to keep our neighbors' sheep from eating recently planted saplings or from getting into Trevor's prized vegetable garden.

One of the neighbors had nine rams (we called them the Naughty Nine), which were experts at finding weak spots in the fencing. They would squeeze through the fence into a patch of oak and ash saplings, munching the leaves that protruded from their protective plastic tubes. The leaves handily consumed, the rams would knock down the protective plastic tubing and the wooden stakes they were zip-tied to in order to finish off the rest of the supple trees, right down to the ground.

One spring a squad of four truant lambs regularly slipped through sagging fence wires, making a beeline

---

12 Barks, The Glance, 79.

for the garden. The invaders would be halfway through two rows of carrots, rubbing their full bellies and burping, before Trevor would discover them. Our chasing the lambs back to their field had all the trappings of a French farce, only replace scantily-clad women slamming bedroom doors with two estate workers encumbered by three layers of clothing topped with swishing outer-layer waterproofs and stumbling on wet hillsides while four lambs evaded capture and ran circles around them.

Every time we discovered truant sheep, we'd have to walk sections of the fence line to find out where the blighters were getting through. When we found the likely spot, we would fix it and congratulate ourselves, only to have to patch a different section a few days later. The better approach would have been to spend the time examining the entire fence perimeter, mark the weak spots on a map, then fix them. *Properly* fix them, not just cobble together some spare parts and pray they held.

If you feel like you're reliving the same nightmare over and over, ignoring or spot-patching the issue isn't the answer. Sometimes you need to tear down what you're doing—literally or figuratively—and start over. Here's another way to look at it: the universe is showing you where the holes are in your approach, your logic, or your attitude. Consider the message a favor and take time to update your method, or your thoughts and feelings about something.

If you're living your life as if fastened to a pole, from that vantage point you will continue to see and do the same things over and over. Untether yourself from your narrow views and discover what it's like from another view. Like the neighbor's truant sheep, free yourself in the infinite pasture.

Chapter 13

Annoyance

When you want a nice bath and there's no hot water.

Translation

Creature comforts elude you; is it too much to ask for a simple thing?

Rumi Verse[13]

How will you know the difficulties of being human if you're always flying off to blue perfection? Where will you plant your grief seeds? Workers need ground to scrape and hoe, not the sky of unspecified perfection.

Unpacking It

As part of the estate team, I worked outside all day every day. In case you're unfamiliar with the weather in Scotland, here's a primer: It's cold and wet much of the year, and especially in autumn and winter. We dressed for it, but that didn't keep the damp cold from seeping into our marrow, stiffening every joint, and leaving us with permanent chapped patches of skin that were hard to protect from the wind hurling cold rain at us. What could possibly be so important to be working outside all day every day in such weather? Taking care of animals, tending to the garden (for us there was no off-season in the garden), and cutting, hauling, and splitting firewood to feed the wood stove that fueled the boiler that heated the water for our bathing needs as well as our dorm rooms.

The dormitory didn't have any bathtubs in the communal bathroom, just showers. The problem was the showers were more misty than showery. It was also hard to get the water temperature right. Adjusting the knobs required a neurosurgeon's precision to find that perfect temperature somewhere between frostbite and steel-forging. You either ended up getting scalded or had to make do with a lukewarm shower. Every day I literally ached for a hot bath in a real tub. But sharing accommodations with forty other

---

13 Barks, *Birdsong*, 38.

people, with only a few bathtubs in the main house to go around, meant having to queue, by which time the hot water was used. At best, my chances of a hot bath were fifty-fifty; my deluded optimism, 100 percent.

One day, my fellow resident and good pal Shane offered the bathtub in his cottage, which he shared with a woman and her young daughter. We had to schedule my bath time when they didn't need it. It would be my first proper tub bath in about a month, so I decided to make the most of it by bringing along special scented bubbles, a loofah, and some votive candles. I packed my things in a little bag and skipped across the dormitory courtyard to Shane's cottage and to warm, watery bliss.

I set the candles around the bathtub's rim and lit them. I turned on the hot and cold water taps, poured in the scented bubbles, got undressed, and climbed into the tub. But the water wasn't quite warm enough yet. I turned off the cold tap to let the hot water catch up. The temperature never got above lukewarm. The only thing worse than being dry and cold is being wet and not as cold, but still not warm. I went back to my room defeated.

A week later Shane offered again. I set my candles on the tub's edge and lit them. But this time, I turned on only the hot water tap. I poured in the bubbles, got undressed, and waited a minute for the water to get hot. And waited. And waited. Pretty soon my goosebumps became goose lumps. Another no-go.

Shane offered a third time. Only I wasn't going to get out the candles or pour the bubbles in or even take my clothes off until hot water was guaranteed. I knelt by the tub, gave the hot water tap the stink eye, and turned it on. Out ran scalding water—hallelujah! I set out the candles, poured in my bubbles, tore off my clothes, and jumped in. Just as I was sinking beneath steaming, wet perfection, Shane's roommate knocked on the door. She insisted that her daughter needed a bath right then and there. No, I couldn't just have twenty minutes; I needed to vacate the tub now. And so it went, always something at communal Braemar.

It seems selfish to expect creature comforts when people all over the world suffer from far greater problems. If you lose your stuffing because you can't get a few simple pleasures, remember that you can't always get what you want when you want it. Are there lesser things you can settle for? Greater things you can forego? Going without from time to time will make you better equipped to handle more serious deprivations, such as being ordered to stay in your house for months to thwart far greater consequences of business as usual during say, a deadly global virus outbreak. You'll also learn to appreciate things more when you do get to have them. How will you know the difficulties of what others could be suffering if life is always perfect for you?

Chapter 14

Annoyance

When endless rains flood your garden shed and rot your Wellington boots.

Translation

You never seem to get a break from life dumping on you.

Rumi Verse[14]

We don't have to follow the pressure flow of wanting. We can be led by the guide. Wishes may or may not come true in this house of disappointment. Let's push the door open together and leave.

Unpacking It

In Scotland it rains nine days out of seven (okay, slight exaggeration; only eight days out of seven). It rains so frequently that when it stops, you appreciate the gray, cloudy sky. The sun does peek out every once in a while, but the first winter I lived at Braemar, the Scottish Borders suffered storm after storm after storm.

One week in January, we had six consecutive days of downpour mixed with drizzle. Even the ducks and geese refused to come out of their shelters for a paddle on the lake. They didn't need to; there was a small lake forming right where they sat. We had to keep the chickens inside their coops because otherwise they would stand in the rain and get soaked, which isn't good for any living creature. We learned our lesson after twice finding dead hens a day or two following a massive downpour (they can suffer from pneumonia). The poor turkeys didn't have any shelters apart for hunkering down under the Leyland hedge. At night they roosted on the chicken coop roofs.

It rained so hard that January week that a wide, shallow river of water poured off the hill in front of the garden shed, pooling on the gravel track at the bottom of the hill. One afternoon I decided to tidy the shed because there wasn't much else to do outside in such weather. The garden shed had three entrances; one was on the side of the long

---

14   Moyne and Barks, Say I Am You, 72.

building and the other two were opposite each other, one opening to the garden and the other opening to the gravel track. Above the gravel track, water had poured down the hill and formed a large pond that extended the length of the forty-foot-long garden shed. I waded through the water, deciding to enter the side door of the shed because water was about a half-foot high all along the front. When I opened the side door, I discovered a torrent of water roiling through the little building. It was flowing through a one-inch gap at the bottom of the shed door that faced the gravel track. The building was shin-deep in muddy water. A dozen plastic pots spun around like teacups on a Disney theme park ride; plastic labels floated like miniature surfboards. I opened the garden-facing door to let the water flow out, taking with it the pots and plant labels. But the water kept pouring in under the opposite door. I tried plugging the gap with various materials such as plastic sheeting, rocks, and wood planks. It didn't work, so I opened the door. Now the garden shed had a creek flowing through it.

My tidying that day consisted of dragging out all of the estate's spare rain and garden wear from under one of the work benches, which was the only place we could store it. It was a jumble of sodden jackets, wellies, gloves, over-trousers, and hats. I wrung out the salvageable clothes and draped them over the handles of the spades that hung from pegs on the wall. Water coursed down the walls from the leaking roof, creating a perpetual growth of green and black mildew and slime on the painted cinderblock walls. Much of the clothing was half-rotted anyway from lying on a perpetually damp concrete floor—and that was before the flood.

During that same January of Our Endless Rain, a visitor from Tasmania dropped in. Eric was the antipodean version of Bear Grylls, only about two decades before Bear

Grylls. For several days, we watched in awe as Eric lent a hand on the estate doing odd jobs such as hauling away boulders that he hoisted onto his shoulders, splitting fifty cords of firewood, and pulling our one-ton tractor out of the mud with his bare hands (okay, slight exaggeration; he wore gloves).

Another job Eric tackled was to help Trevor and two young men who were studying at Braemar dig a three-foot-deep by thirty-foot-long trench to lay piping for a new water spigot in the garden. And by "help," I mean Eric dug the trench while the other three guys watched. They had to get out of his way because Eric worked so hard and fast, anyone within six feet of his slinging shovel would have been in the firing line of mud. During one particular day that it poured buckets, Eric decided rather than getting his clothes wet while digging the miniature version of the Suez Canal, he'd just take them off. For a couple of hours Bear Eric, with his ripped chest and arms, pick-axed and dug in nothing but undershorts in the near-freezing Scottish monsoon. Suddenly, my interest in garden trench-digging was piqued.

While I'm not suggesting you remove your clothes to cope with life's curveballs (although if that helps and you won't get arrested, go for it!), sometimes you have to go with the downpour's flow. Eric's was a classic case of if you can't beat them—or control the weather—join them. Rain schmain, it wasn't going to stop him or ruin his day, especially because he knew he had absolutely no control over it.

As Rumi says, if you feel a constant sense of disappointment in your "house," your world, then leave it behind—metaphorically speaking, or maybe even literally. We may or may not get our wish for perpetual blue skies and sunshine. I've said it in other places in this book: expectation is the gateway to disappointment. If you're hanging out in the house of disappointment, time to find a new place to live. Learn to work with what you can't control. Learn to mitigate potential problems or at least reduce the inevitable damage. If there's a chance your wellies will rot, store them somewhere they're not likely to get wet. More often than I should have, I let the gray days depress me. I'd get angry at the sky for raining, which is like being angry at water for being wet. Eventually, I found ways to cope. After all, I chose to live in Scotland. Enjoying the company of my fellow Braemarites helped ease the stress as did accepting that sometimes I got dumped on. Accept what you can't change and carry on.

Chapter 15

Annoyance

....

When you're the only hard worker among a bunch of slackers.

Translation

....

Resentment is eating away at your soul.

Rumi Verse[15]

Anyone who sees their own faults before noticing those of others, why don't they correct themselves? People of the world don't look at themselves, and so they blame another.

Unpacking It

Volunteering in a communal setting can be a gold mine for those who don't feel guilty enjoying the fruits of everyone else's labor. Let's call them Leeches. Volunteering in a communal setting can be a toxic environment for those who go well beyond earning their keep, toiling from sunrise to well after sundown because they just want to *get 'er done*. Let's call those people Martyrs. Volunteering in a communal setting can be a fantastic experience for those who know their boundaries and don't work themselves to death. Extra points for not letting the Leeches and Martyrs get to them. Let's call those people Goldilocks.

My mother and preacher father raised their children to work hard, but it was less about idleness and the devil than it was about believing everything could always be improved upon. Also, we were trained to put others first, which is the perfect way to prime your offspring for volunteer work. I have volunteered a lot throughout my life, rarely turning down a request to pitch in. My perfectionist attitude, sprinkled with a little control freak, meant I was the first up at dawn digging into whatever needed doing and the last to call it a day. I took my duties seriously and wore my exhaustion as a badge of honor. Braemar loved me. Until the badge of exhaustion began weighing me down. In case you hadn't guessed, I belonged to the

---

15 Helminksi and Helminski, Rumi Daylight, 119.

tribe of Martyrs.

I chose the difficult path to realizing that being one of the harder-working volunteers wasn't always a good thing. In part, the point of Braemar was learning to serve with gratitude and humbleness. Our work there, whether it was baking bread, raking leaves, or cleaning toilets, was an act of service to one another and ultimately to God. All residents, regardless of our assigned purpose, were expected to help where needed and called. Martyrs and Goldilocks folk responded to the call, while Leeches benefited from the literal blood, sweat, and tears of the rest of us. Not only did this annoy me, it fed my resentment. When you're full of resentment, however (ahem, Martyrs), no amount of service for a good cause can make you feel better.

I spent many hours working while holding anger and resentment toward others in my heart. Although those "others," the Leeches, numbered only a few, to me they may as well have been an army of thousands. One day I was so incensed by the Leeches being leeches, that I accidentally pulled up a bunch of flowers from the garden thinking they were weeds. I hadn't been paying attention, consumed with vengeful thoughts. Another similarly vengeful experience resulted in me shouting at people as I stormed away from the lunch table (see Chapter 21).

Yes, my tendency to overdo it was a self-imposed burden. Whereas the Goldilocks folk knew their limits—when to stop in deference to self-care—I rushed from one task to the next. I didn't know when to call it a day or let good enough be enough. Braemar was trying to teach me that the quality of the action, and the thoughts while doing it, mattered much more than the quantity of boxes ticked as completed.

Know your limits. If you have a tendency to overdo it, before committing to anything, establish how much and in what ways you will participate. Confirm how many hours you will work and what work you will and won't do and then communicate those boundaries with those who need to know. What good are points for a job well done that kills you or prevents you from enjoying life? If someone pressures you to do more, weigh the consequences. If doing more might create anger or resentment, politely decline. But don't blame others if you fail to enforce your boundaries. Likewise, don't expect others to know what those boundaries are if you don't tell them. First take a look at your own faults and correct them before getting angry at others for being who they are.

Chapter 16

Annoyance

When the work never gets done.

Translation

You wonder what "there" looks like, but you can't ever get "there" to find out.

Rumi Verse[16]

The discovery of treasure is by luck and even more, it is rare. One must earn a living so long as the body is able. Does earning a livelihood prevent the discovery of treasure? Don't retire from work; that treasure, indeed, follows after the work.

Unpacking It

Braemar occupied roughly two hundred acres of land and included a twenty-two-room house, a handful of cottages, a large dormitory, a massive vegetable garden and border gardens, several outbuildings, and livestock. During the two years I lived there, a rotating roster of residents from all over the world shared meals, living and sleeping space, and bathrooms. At any given time the residents numbered from as few as seven to as many as forty-five or so. That didn't include holidays and events when our numbers temporarily swelled to more than a hundred.

Keeping everyone, including the livestock, fed and sheltered while running spiritual study courses meant no shortage of tasks to be done. Think of how much maintenance your own place requires then multiply your household and family responsibilities by a hundred and you have Braemar. Also consider that the house and some of the buildings were more than two hundred years old. In some ways built to last; in other ways, a maintenance hell hole.

Here is a shortlist of just *some* of my shared responsibilities with Trevor: cutting down trees, chopping them up, and splitting firewood; mucking out poultry coops and pens, feeding, and tending to poultry; fixing fences and chasing sheep; clearing up yard debris and doing lawn

---

16   Helminksi and Helminski, Rumi Daylight, 112.

care; compost spreading, planting, weeding, harvesting an acre of garden space; trimming hedges, planting and caring for thousands of trees; fixing potholes in the half-mile-long driveway and tending to numerous drainage issues. And these were just the jobs we could always count on having to do, to say nothing of the multitude of tasks that unexpectedly cropped up, forcing us to deal with them in the moment. I also helped wash dishes after every meal and tea break and sometimes helped prepare meals, prepare rooms for guests, and helped Rafi, our maintenance man, with odd jobs.

After many months of trying to get it all done so I could rest, I learned the hard way that there is *never a time when everything is all done*. Never. I also wasted a lot of energy being angry at the Leeches and Goldilocks because I didn't know when to rest (see Chapter 15). At one point in my experience I had to retreat from my Braemar retreat just to get a break.

Sometimes I fantasize about what it would be like not to have any chores to do, only the things I want to do. (When I become wealthy enough to hire a full-time personal assistant, cook, gardener, maintenance person, and cleaner, I'll let you know what it's like.)

On the other hand, maybe the goal isn't to reach some presumed end. What if the goal is facing challenges with determination; accepting hardship as a way to make you stronger; doing your daily tasks with thankfulness that you even have a house and food; allowing grace to push you through the difficult parts; and knowing when to rest? According to Rumi, this is where we discover our treasure. In doing work, in dealing with everyday life, in interacting with others we learn about ourselves and the world. This is treasure. Life will always require effort, and stuff will always get in the way while you're busy living. So there really is no *there*; only *here and now* (death excepted).

Chapter 17

Annoyance

When you get a mouthful of dirty fish tank water.

Translation

You sometimes resent caring for others.

Rumi Verse[17]

Love is the way messengers from the mystery tell us things. Love is the mother. We are her children. She shines inside us, visible–invisible, as we trust or lose trust, or feel it start to grow again.

Unpacking It

We members of the Braemar community were expected to care for one another. In a general sense, this meant everyone had assigned work to ensure that we were all kept fed and housed and to ensure things ran smoothly. In a specific sense, it meant when you were ill, someone brought a tray of food to your room at mealtimes. Or when you were struggling with emotional issues that inevitably arose under the living, working, and studying circumstances, someone was there to listen. We were also all expected to participate in ablution day, which was every Thursday. On ablution day we all participated in cleaning the manor house and dormitory. There were also abluting tasks in the garden and maintenance buildings and on the house grounds.

One of my many responsibilities was looking after the non-human creatures of various speciation, including all manner of poultry, sheep, and the occasional semi-feral cat. These things in themselves required regular ablution, especially the poultry. Every week I and the students on the Braemar Course pitched mucky straw out of the duck pens and chicken coops and spread fresh bedding. We also scrubbed the coops on hands and knees with a brush. We hauled buckets of hot, soapy water from the laundry room to the chicken field, where the coops were. My head had

---

17 Barks, Soul of Rumi, 33.

scabs from where I'd bumped into nails protruding from the low ceilings. We shifted tons of sodden straw in wheelbarrows to the garden compost and scrubbed slime from the ducks' water basins. The garden spigots froze in winter, so to get water for the waterfowl pens, I would stomp through the ice on the edge of the lake to fill a bucket. I also had to clear a path through the ice so the ducks and geese could access the ice-free zone in the middle of the lake.

Caring for all these creatures, human and non-human, was exhausting and messy. Sometimes I wished the animals could just take care of themselves. Then fish duty landed in my lap. We had a half-dozen fish that lived in a large tank in the bay window of the servery. (For my American friends, a servery is a small room typically between the kitchen and dining room; a feature of manor homes that can afford staff. Braemar's servery is where we stored our dishware and eating utensils and washed dishes.) It was mesmerizing to watch our finned friends while we stood at the sink washing and drying dishes by hand.

Because we kept the tank in the window, the sunlight sped up algae growth. The tank had to be cleaned at least biweekly, if not weekly. This required netting the fish and keeping them in a bucket so their tank water could be drained and replaced. I had to climb up onto the sink and sit on the drain board, or stand in the sink, to reach the tank. To drain it, I had to put one end of half-inch-diameter plastic tubing in the bottom of the tank and siphon the water up and out the other end. Siphoning required sucking really hard; imagine sucking on a large-diameter straw from a thirty-gallon tank to get the water up the tubing. I would turn blue from several attempts of almost getting it there before letting go because of light-headedness. I could never get the timing right, either. If I took my mouth off the tubing too soon, the water would drop back down into the tank. If I didn't take my mouth off soon enough, I'd get a mouthful of manky fish water. I usually waited too long. (Years later I learned another technique for siphoning that didn't involve sucking on a tube.)

It was awkward sitting on the stainless steel drainboard and twisting every which way to reach inside the tank and remove the little sunken castle, diving man, rocks, and fake seaweed. I'd have to scrub the slime off those things and the sides of the tank, rinse the gravel with clean water, and siphon that out too. Come to think of it, a lot of my work involved cleaning up the poo left behind by others.

Caretaking is messy. Yet, as beings created in love, we are called to love others. Rumi notes love is the mother and we are her children. You may lose trust from time to time in that association, but when you let love shine inside you, you will feel it grow again.

I often griped about my animal care jobs, yet I loved all the animals entrusted to my care, even if they didn't return the affection. Eventually, I changed my attitude. Instead of a chore to muddle through, I chose to accept caretaking as a privilege, an opportunity to demonstrate my love for others that depended on me. In time, that attitude even extended to my human housemates.

Chapter 18

Annoyance

When no one volunteers to make tea and cakes.

Translation

Others let you down.

Rumi Verse[18]

If you are irritated by every rub, how will your mirror be polished?

Unpacking It

Many centuries ago much of Great Britain's native hard-wood forests were felled to build ships for the navy. Trees were also cut down to build dwellings and furniture, as well as to use for cooking, heating, conveyances, tools, and a great many other things. In the early twentieth century, to make up for the inevitable tree shortfall, Sitka spruce were planted in large swaths of straight rows. The species isn't native to Britain even though spruce plantations account for much of the forests. Spruce grows fast in the wet climate, but they create biological deserts; not much good for wildlife, and not much grows in the understory.

So what does all this have to do with making tea and cakes? You could say that because the British cut down most of their forests hundreds of years ago, I had the opportunity to help reforest Braemar's little patch of Scotland.

Braemar decided to make a party of planting seventeen thousand trees. Over a two-week period in April, for two years, they invited everyone on their mailing list to help. Of the few thousand at the time, a hundred or so Braemarites, along with families and friends, came to volunteer. They didn't stop at just two years, though. The Annual Tree Bash, as it became known, lasted for many years afterward, in which volunteers came to continue planting trees and to care for the saplings from years past.

Having only a two-week window in which to plant

---

18   Helminksi and Helminski, Rumi Daylight, 69.

thousands of trees on hilly—and sometimes boggy—ground, is physically demanding and requires careful planning. Because Braemar relied on volunteers, Trevor and I had to make sure they were happy. Breaking for morning coffee and afternoon teatime was essential (besides being utterly British). Caffeine and sweets proved to be great motivators for convincing tree planters to continue working day after day in often ugly weather.

In helping to manage the project, I made sure all the trees were planted properly—a multi-pronged feat in itself—and that the house staff were informed about the volunteers. Staff needed to know who was arriving, when, and how long they were staying in order to prepare dorm rooms and the appropriate amount of food. Because the volunteers outnumbered the staff ten to one, I had to ask the tree planters to support the house staff to support the tree planters. During the first week, we worked like a well-oiled machine. During the second week, the volunteer makeup changed; the more-eager, hard workers went home, leaving fewer people who were willing to help out with household duties such as cooking and cleaning.

We were short on people willing to prepare the daily tea and coffee, plus bake fresh goodies for the famished volunteers. The job fell on me after I got tired of begging tree planters to help with this task. I still also had hundreds of other tree planting things to do every day. There's only so much one person can handle before having a breakdown (see Chapter 19).

I felt let down by pretty much everyone. Before the tree planting party started, we staff had a big meeting to plan the details. The house staff had promised they would take care of all the support; I was not to worry. During week two, however, Braemar's leader attended a conference in England, taking three of the essential house staff with him and leaving the rest of us shorthanded. The few staff left behind felt the crush of feeding, housing, and cleaning up after the volunteers. They decided to put in only so many hours and then call it quits for the day. A few were angry that the volunteers weren't pitching in more to wash dishes and make tea and coffee, for example, a legitimate complaint. I also felt let down by the tree planters, who seemed to think preparing tea and cakes either beneath them or a job they shouldn't have to do, despite that they understood the Braemar Way: everyone pitches in where and when called. And finally, I felt let down by Trevor, who decided that his garden was more important and spent long days there instead of helping with the tree planting.

There was a lot of blame to go around, yet in the end I learned that people will always let me down from time to time, even if expectations are reasonable and agreed upon. More useful than getting upset is not relying too heavily on others in the first place. Circumstances change and people can back out of commitments for whatever reason. Maybe you find unknown strengths in yourself when others let you down. Also, sometimes letting things "fail" can have positive outcomes. After two days of rushing to prepare refreshments because nobody else would, the volunteers suffered sufficiently enough to help me (see Chapter 34).

Others will let you down at some point. Have a backup plan—or two or three—and be prepared to handle the situation yourself, minus the bad feelings, which never come to much good. If you are irritated by every rub, how will you be polished into an increasingly better—and potentially happier—version of yourself?

Chapter 19

Annoyance

When people steal your Kit Kat stash, causing you to have a breakdown.

Translation

You're making too much of a little thing; your priorities are misplaced.

Rumi Verse[19]

Essence is emptiness; everything else accidental.
Emptiness brings peace to your loving. Everything
else, disease. In this world of trickery, emptiness is
what your soul wants.

Unpacking It

When I agreed to help Braemar with its ambitious tree-planting project, I had no idea how many details were involved in organizing more than a hundred volunteers over two weeks to plant thousands of trees (see Chapter 18). I took it upon myself to manage tree-related logistics as well as coordinate the support staff, often going out of my way to get jobs done that should have been left for others (first mistake). I made it my mission to ensure everyone's happiness (second mistake). Part of keeping the volunteer tree planters happy was feeding them goodies during tea and coffee breaks. Sugar-laden treats not only maximized their calorie intake for the difficult outdoor labor, especially when the sleet was lashing down, but goodies persuaded people—especially the teenaged boys and young men among the ranks—to get out of bed. Trevor told me that the previous year's tree planting volunteers had been particularly motivated by a large supply of Kit Kats that one of the volunteers had brought with him. Apparently, this man had worked for the company that made Kit Kats. Because the chocolate bars had been a big hit, I was strongly encouraged to augment our home-baked goodies with the well-loved treats.

Maybe it was the abundance of young people with ravenous appetites and metabolisms, but we started going

---

19   Barks, Birdsong, 22.

through a lot of Kit Kats just in the first week of the two-week event. Braemar's head cook informed me these were too expensive and we'd have to start rationing them. Well tell that to the young people who were busting their behinds in all kinds of weather out there planting trees! Since the cook was also the person in charge of the food budget, I had little choice but to abide. Besides that, we had lost our head baker so we didn't have any more fresh-baked goodies. To make up for it, the cook bought cheap cookies and cakes. The volunteers started to complain, and I was afraid they'd stop showing up to plant trees.

To ration them, I hid the remaining Kit Kat stash. But the young people—who raided the kitchen pantry every night—discovered the hiding place. I found another hiding spot for the remaining candy bars, and then another and another. With just a few days to go until the end of the planting, I went to the pantry one morning to check how many Kit Kats we had. I needed to know rationing numbers for that afternoon's tea break. When I opened the tin, all I saw was my reflection staring back at me. The Kit Kats were gone. Nada. Zip. Zilch.

How did I react? I did what any self-respecting mature adult would do and let it go without another thought. Kidding! I had a breakdown right there in the pantry holding an empty biscuit tin, sobbing and cursing. Yes, I totally lost it because some kids had eaten some candy bars, which were meant for them in the first place. To be fair, I was under a lot of stress from organizing the event, so my coping skills had already headed south. Nonetheless, would the volunteers have really stopped planting trees if they didn't get their coveted treats? Trying to control munchie syndrome in teenage boys and twenty-something men, what was I thinking?

If worry about trivial matters is driving you mental, time to take stock of priorities. Of course, if it's important to you, it must not be trivial, right? Maybe, maybe not. Ask yourself why that particular thing is important. Why does it matter? What's the worst that could happen if your worries actually manifested? The essence of peace is not to allow your energy to be drained by unimportant things. Filling yourself with worry, especially with matters that are trivial in the greater picture, serves nothing but anxiety and dis-ease. If your soul is beleaguered, feed it with a little emptiness, for peace' sake.

Chapter 20

Annoyance

....

When children use your grain bucket for
collecting frog spawn.

Translation

....

Others don't respect the rules, or maybe you just
need to lighten up.

Rumi Verse[20]

Today, like every other day, we wake up empty and frightened. Don't open the door to the study and begin reading. Take down a musical instrument. Let the beauty we love be what we do. There are hundreds of ways to kneel and kiss the ground.

Unpacking It

During my time at Braemar, five children from ages eighteen months to nine years lived there with their parents. Other children periodically visited with their families, including Trevor's two children. I would have given anything to grow up at Braemar. What child wouldn't love having this vast estate of forests, pastures, gardens, ponds, and animals for a kingdom? In addition, there were all these adults to adore you and the big manor house to sneak into, where you could snitch cookies and cakes from the pantry. There were the barn, the old sawmill, and dormitory to explore even though you weren't allowed to but you still did occasionally when adults weren't looking.

For some reason, children adore me, even though I never wanted to have any of my own. Shortly after I arrived at Braemar, the children decided they wanted to hang out with me as much as possible. Maybe it was because I was a pushover for letting them do things they probably shouldn't have been doing, such as drive the tractor (sitting on my lap). They always wanted to "help" me do my work. Their offer was sweet and well-intended, but it usually made more work for me or delayed me in accomplishing anything at all. And if you read this far into the book, you know that I am all about getting

---

20 Moyne and Barks, Open Secret, 7.

everything done!

One task the kids loved helping me with was taking care of the turkeys, chickens, ducks, and geese. In addition to feeding, watering, and mucking out all the poultry shelters, I had to round up the ducks and geese from the lake and herd them into their pens every night. This was achieved by bribing them with food. We kept a tightly sealed garbage bin full of barley by the pens near the lake. I would fill a bucket with the grain and shake it while calling to the birds to come in. My feathered friends and I had the routine down pretty well.

Whenever they got a chance, the kids wanted to help me round them up. The trouble was the birds were spooked by the children's high-pitched squeals and general darting around and boisterousness. So I'd have to shoo the kids away before trying to get the naturally skittish birds to come in from the lake. If you don't have kids, you might be thinking *why didn't you just tell the kids to be quiet?* (to which I would respond with hearty laughter). If you do have kids, that question would never pop into your mind.

In the spring, the kids liked to collect copious amounts of frog spawn from the lakeshore to do whatever kids do with copious amounts of frog spawn. And what better container to use than the grain bucket conveniently located near the lake by the waterfowl pens? Many spring nights when it was time to feed the birds and put them away, I'd have to search for the bucket. When I couldn't find it, I had to search for another container to put the barley in. In the morning, I had to scold the children for taking my bucket and make them promise never to do it again. They would promise, and the next evening the same routine would repeat itself (bucket missing, look for another container, scold children, etc.).

The children got up to other things too, such as not returning borrowed hand tools from the garden shed, making off with wheelbarrows, and sneaking into my room when I wasn't there to look at the incubating poultry eggs. Clearly, establishing some rules was required, such as *no touching the garden tools without adult supervision, leave things where you found them*, and *stay out of my room*. Yeah right; as if *that* worked!

Items continued to disappear or I would find the egg incubator tampered with or I'd eventually find my hat—after two days of searching—on a child's head (she just wanted a little piece of me because she loved me!). So much for the rules. A change of tactic was in order. I got *two* other buckets for the children just for frog spawn and started hiding the grain bucket in a place where I could grab it on my way to pen the birds at night. I designated "special children tools" just for their little patch of garden and appeased them by telling them that no adults were allowed to use the children's tools. As for the egg incubator, I told them that if they kept disturbing the eggs, the baby chicks would die inside the shells. Sometimes guilt works (and it was the truth).

The grain bucket still disappeared occasionally (after all, three buckets were better than two!), and sometimes our tools were ferried off by little hands on some great adventure to explore the outer universe. I learned to live with it because in the bigger picture, what's a little inconvenience compared with a child's curiosity to learn, play, and thrive?

If others are flouting your rules or exasperating you into a constant state of impatience, develop a hack for that. Find a new hiding spot for items that tend to go missing or buy another one and designate "mine" and "yours." You could try explaining the reason behind your rules; if it's convincing enough, maybe your perceived offenders will understand and show respect. On the other hand, are your rules too strict? What *are* your reasons for them and can you let them go? Re-assess or learn to hack or live with the minor inconveniences. Rumi invites us to take time to enjoy the simple pleasures of life instead of always being about business—the rules. Let the beauty you love be what you do. Give a little, lighten up. There are hundreds of ways to kneel and kiss the ground, hundreds of ways to be thankful for and enjoy this beautiful world, collecting frog spawn among them.

Chapter 21

Annoyance

When someone eats your onions but not your garlic.

Translation

Your needs are not others' priority; you want sympathy, but it's not coming.

Rumi Verse[21]

Anger and lust make us squint; they cloud the spirit so it strays from truth. When self-interest appears, virtue hides: a hundred veils rise between the heart and the eye.

Unpacking It

When you live communally with other people, you're more vulnerable to illness. Coughs and sniffles and more serious ailments are easily spread in places where dishes are washed by hand and dried with the same towels used for drying hands. Braemar was such a place, and I got ill frequently, mostly with minor head colds. A few times a more serious ailment landed me in bed for several days.

To keep illness at bay back home, I used to soak raw garlic in honey and drink the juices. Turns out Braemar used the same home remedy but substituted onion for garlic because garlic was forbidden in our cooking. The reason, someone gave me, was that garlic scared the angels away. Who knew? Years later, other Braemarites disputed that, claiming garlic in our cooking would not have gone unnoticed during the nightly moving meditation the students practiced (see Chapter 25), which made everyone sweaty. Whatever the reason, garlic was forbidden in the house.

During one particularly exhausting week just before Christmas, I was working twelve-hour days to keep up with household chores that had backed up because of a water shortage (see Chapter 33). Getting ill was inevitable, so I gave Braemar's remedy a try. I left my diced onions soaking in honey in a bowl, covering them in plastic wrap

---

21 Helminksi and Helminski, Rumi Daylight, 24.

and taping a note to the bowl asking others not to touch. When I returned later to drink it, it was gone; the cook had put my honeyed onions in the lunch. I was furious. Just before that, I had screamed at a tableful of people for being Leeches (see Chapter 15). During that week we really needed as many extra hands as possible to help prepare for the arrival of more than one hundred house guests for the holidays. Many of the residents were on a pilgrimage in Turkey, part of the Braemar course (see Chapter 27), so we were shorthanded. However, of those of us who didn't go to Turkey that year, not everyone was as eager as me to assist with the accumulating household chores. Further, no one seemed to care that I was on death's door with a bad sinus infection yet still dragged myself out of bed to help make a dent in the mountains of household laundry. Where was my well-deserved sympathy?

Celeste, a fellow resident, came to check on me in my room, where I had stormed off to after learning that the cook had used my illness remedy. Celeste sat on the edge of my bed and listened while I'll complained about how much I was working and how little others were. When I was finished, she reminded me of the Biblical tale of Mary and Martha. The sisters had invited Jesus to their house for supper, and while Martha scrambled around making things nice for their exalted house guest—preparing all the food and doing all the work—Mary sat at Jesus' feet and enjoyed his company. This pissed Martha off. She told Jesus to tell Mary to get off her fat lazy behind and help out. Jesus told Martha to chillax.

Celeste reminded me of the story's moral: "There are more important things than running around all busy-like. Don't let your service to others distract you from the ultimate reason for your work, which is to contemplate God. What good are you to this community if your service is tainted with resentment?"

Celeste told me to get some rest; that the work would get done; that people would step in when they were ready and able.

I don't recommend revenge as a problem-solver or field-leveler, but at that particular time, it seemed like a good idea. So I drove into town and bought some raw garlic to make a new concoction. I hadn't actually planned to eat it, though. I hoped that the cook would use it in a meal, thereby "poisoning" everyone with the forbidden fruit and scaring the angels away and in general wreaking havoc on the entire Braemar household. But that never happened because after having read the cook the riot act for using my onions, he was sufficiently afraid of crossing my path again. I don't know which made me more annoyed, that he used my onions the first time or that he *didn't* use my garlic the second time.

Assuming you're a fully functioning adult, only one person in this world is ever going to care 100 percent about you, and that is *you* (and maybe your parents). Is it time to stop feeling sorry for yourself and expecting others to as well? Don't let veils, (a.k.a., obstacles of the mind) come between your heart and your eyes. Anger and resentment are two human emotions that have the power to destroy people—and not just those that harbor it, but everyone in their wake. Loving and serving others requires both action and contemplation; knowing when to work and knowing when to rest. Superheroes need not apply; just regular people. Serve others out of gratitude and willingness, never resentment. In my case, I later found out that some of the people I had labeled as Leeches were actually contributing—just in ways I hadn't noticed. That was me humbled.

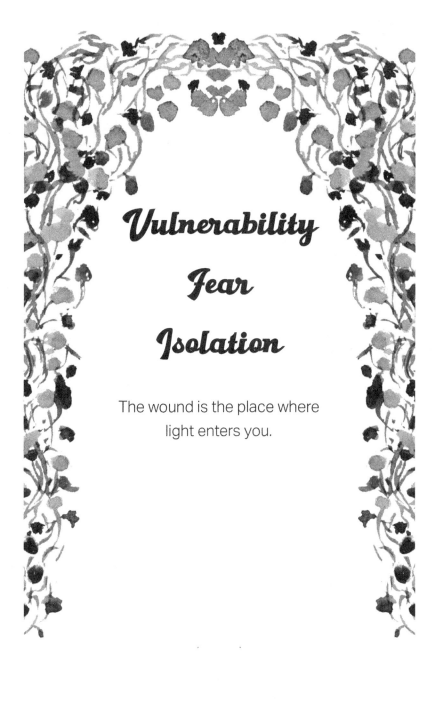

Vulnerability

Fear

Isolation

The wound is the place where
light enters you.

Chapter 22

Annoyance

When your train never arrives.

Translation

You feel thwarted from the start.

Rumi Verse[22]

Try not to resist the changes that come your way. Instead let life live through you. And do not worry that your life is turning upside down. How do you know that the side you are used to is better than the one to come?

Unpacking It

My plans were solid. From Barnes Bridge Station in West London, I would take the train to Euston Station. At Euston I would board another train north to Carlisle, England, just south of the Scotland border. In Carlisle I would board a bus to my final destination of Eltondean, the town near Braemar House. My connections weren't necessarily tight, but they didn't leave a whole lot of room for error. The only problem was my first train never arrived. I waited thirty minutes past the time when the train was supposed to have arrived, uncertain whether it was an actual delay or a matter of reduced service for whatever reason that Monday morning.

I used to be easily annoyed by a change in plans (see Chapter 1). In this case, I was especially upset because it involved a long journey carefully timed and stitched together with expensive train tickets. It was a classic domino situation: missing one train would lead to missed connections downstream. It's bad enough when it happens at home, but in a foreign country it's worse because you are in unfamiliar territory. If you have local friends, you could call them and beg them to put you up for one more night. If not, you would have to find other accommodations. Alternatively, you have to take a later train—paying more

---

22 AZ Quotes, https://www.azquotes.com/quote/512593.

money—and arrive at your destination late, where people are expecting you, but you don't have their number to call and tell them about the delay. (This was pre-cell-phone days for me)

This particular time, I ran to a nearby street corner to catch a bus to the nearest London Underground station, where I bought a ticket to Euston. I sweated it out the whole ride there, which included thirteen stops and a line change. I arrived at Euston, drenched in sweat, a few minutes after my train to Carlisle was supposed to have departed. Thankfully, the gods intervened to delay that train. Not so thankfully, I didn't find that out until after paying a lot of money for a ticket on the next train to Carlisle scheduled for many hours later. So in the end, I boarded my original train at Euston, but it wasn't smooth sailing yet.

When I arrived at Carlisle a few hours later, I still had to get to the bus station to catch my bus to Eltondean, Scotland. When I asked someone at the train station for directions to the bus station, he obliged. But it was a mile away, and I was on foot. I practically ran the entire way, with a backpack on my back and a large camera case strapped to my front. When I got to the bus station, I asked a driver which was the bus to Eltondean. You know what he said? That particular bus actually departed from the train station! And it was leaving in 20 minutes. So I ran the mile back to the bus station, arriving just as the Eltondean bus was pulling away. I flagged down the driver, who stopped for me. Exhausted from both the mental and physical stress of trying to catch transportation, I arrived at all my destinations on time, thanks to a delayed train and a sympathetic bus driver.

Chapter 1 deals with changed plans. Chapter 18 promotes having a backup plan. Both of these situations apply to missed connections. Know your options and do your best to switch gears when necessary. Sometimes high gear is called for, if you can handle it. Sometimes low gear is best—that is, giving way to alternatives might even prove better for you in the long run. Backup plans never hurt nor does knowing that missing something (like a train) isn't usually a big deal. What's more important is arriving safely at your destination.

Have you experienced times when everything you're trying to accomplish is thwarted at every turn? Have you ever thought "Fine, I quit!" and then quit? Have you ever wondered how things might have turned out had you *not* quit and then nagged yourself for doing so and harbored resentment about it? (If not, and you can claim to be a perfectly fulfilled person, I want to learn your secret.) We all suffer from a lack of trust from time to time, but where it really hurts is when we give up on grand plans. The ego has a lot to do with it. It tells us it's better to be safe than sorry. It warns us about perceived hurts and dangers; that's its job. However, the ego can be an overbearing parent, warning us of dangers that don't really exist or making us believe that something is dangerous when it's not (like new experiences). Egos want to *know* without uncertainty; the unknown freaks the ego out. The problem is, we have no way of knowing how something is going to turn out until we try it!

Doubt is normal. Falling down is normal. Being afraid of the unknown is normal. But, as Rumi says, if you resist the changes that come your way—including setbacks—instead of letting life live through you, how will you know that the side you are used to, that is, life as you're living it now, is better than the one to come? And do not worry that your life is turning upside down. If you never overcame doubt; if you never got back up after falling; if you never looked your fears in their mean little faces and said, "Get outta my way!" what is the point? Rumi also says that we are born with potential, goodness, and trust; ideals, dreams, and greatness. *You were born with wings. You are not meant for crawling, so don't. You have wings. Learn to use them and fly.*

I believe that God had a hand in making sure I got to my destination that first day I arrived at Braemar and also in complicating my path. Maybe She was teaching me a lesson in patience, reliance, perseverance, and trust. I had had serious doubts and fears about going to Braemar in the first place. Had I missed any of my connections, I might have changed my mind and turned around, never experiencing Braemar at all. My experience changed my life in amazing ways I never would have known had I given up.

Chapter 23

Annoyance

When you don't understand the jargon or speak the language.

Translation

You feel left out or isolated.

Rumi Verse[23]

If ten lamps are present in one place, each differs in form from another; yet you can't distinguish whose radiance is whose when you focus on the light. In the field of spirit there is no division; no individuals exist. [...] Help this headstrong self disintegrate; that beneath it you may discover unity, like a buried treasure.

Unpacking It

Braemar's courses in esoteric spiritual matters centered on the twelfth-century Muslim scholar and Sufi mystic Ibn Arabi. Because his texts can be heavy-going, and obscure in some ways, they are best studied in a group that includes at least one person who has expert-level understanding of Ibn Arabi's works. When discussing Ibn Arabi and the nature of God, Braemarites would often use the language in the translated texts, which was somewhat archaic. To me it sounded convoluted, like jargon, and I didn't get what people were talking about. Why couldn't they just speak in plain English? They were especially fond of using this spirit-speak when trying to encourage me to take the Braemar study courses or to answer questions I had about their understanding of God. When I asked for an explanation of "the speak," some Braemarites would respond with a condescending smile and say, "If you took the course, you'd understand."

The jargon came across as arrogant and judgmental. It didn't help sell Braemar's studies to me when I first arrived, nor did it enlighten my understanding, which was rather the point of asking questions. Instead, it made me

---

23 Helminksi and Helminski, Rumi Daylight, 28.

feel isolated, an outsider in the community.

I'm a no-nonsense person; I like plain language that everyone can understand, especially when the knowledge is meant for everyone. For many years I have made a living rewriting company jargon into plain language. Years ago as a journalist, I interviewed a lot of people, sometimes about hot-button topics, with whose viewpoints I didn't share. Some interviewees didn't have much of an education; some felt intimidated by me; others tried to intimidate *me*; and some clearly didn't like journalists or the "liberal trash newspaper" that I wrote for. In order to get a good, honest interview, I had to win trust. I found the quickest way to do that was by speaking the language of my interview subjects. That is, I made an effort to understand what was important to them. I did this by asking friendly questions about themselves, empathizing with their concerns, and showing an interest in them personally. I talked to them using their words, including foul language if it made them feel heard. It was genuine on my part; I wasn't just playing them up to get a good story.

At Braemar, I learned to avoid asking certain people questions, relying instead on those who would break down the esoterica into words and examples I understood. Over time and through exposure, I got it, at least a broad understanding of Ibn Arabi's works. When one lives at Braemar, even just as volunteer staff and not as a student on the course, the essence of the studies eventually seeps in.

If you play the part of the jargon speaker, understand that the quickest way to the buried treasure of another soul that Rumi writes about is to speak in a language they understand. This is especially important if you are communicating information that could benefit your conversation partner. If you feel isolated, have patience. Either those isolating you are unaware—in which case tell them how you feel—or they are doing so deliberately because they are ignorant in the ways of human connection. We are all full of bright light—Spirit—regardless of the size, shape, and style of lamp that contains our light. And we shine even brighter together as one great light, indistinguishable as individuals. Keep this knowledge in your heart whenever you feel isolated—and also when you are the one who risks being the isolator.

Chapter 24

Annoyance

When you get zapped by an electric fence.

Translation

The unexpected is shocking; you fail to pay attention to obvious warnings.

Rumi Verse[24]

> *The wise person, in the hour of calamity they took*
> *every precaution to avert, takes warning from the*
> *death of friends.*

Unpacking It

When Trevor and I first met, I wondered whether we would get along. He started out with a sullen demeanor; he wasn't very expressive either. His was the opposite of my somewhat extroverted nature and attempts to have fun while we slogged our tails off in the cold, rainy climes of Scotland. For the first couple of weeks, we mostly worked in silence. We were short on much-needed firewood to heat the water that heated the dormitory, so we spent several days hauling, splitting, and stacking wood. Trevor's soft voice, combined with a British accent, made it difficult for me to understand him clearly.

At the breakfast table he would tell me the jobs for the day, but I was too embarrassed to keep asking him to repeat himself. So I just followed him around on the estate and jumped in to help with whatever the task. Occasionally, I would make a joke (he never laughed) or ask him questions about himself. If he responded at all, his response was usually delayed and spare (*Do you have children?* Wait several seconds. *Yeah.*). Trying to get this man to talk—or even smile—was more exhausting than the actual physical labor we were doing.

One day everything changed. Trevor and I were fixing an old fence at the edge of the property where the neighbor's sheep had been squeezing through the sagging barbed wire. Once loose on our property, the sheep would

---

24   Helminksi and Helminski, Rumi Daylight, 73.

help themselves to the delicious smorgasbord of young trees that a former estate manager had planted a few years earlier and which were struggling to survive. A single strand of smooth wire at the top attached to ceramic insulator caps was a tell-tale sign that the wire was electrified. Trevor seemed rather nonchalant about working near it. He jiggled one of the rotting posts the wire was attached to, trying to determine whether it was worth replacing or better off just securing better. The wire bounced frightfully close to his face. I warned him that it was hot. He laughed, "This wire couldn't carry a current if it wanted to. Look at the state of it! Hasn't worked in years."

To prove his point, Trevor grabbed the smooth wire. Guess what happened? After exclaiming a few choice words, he humbly said, "Um, excuse me a minute. I'll just go have a word with the farmer"—the farmer being the fence owner and controller of the electricity.

In response, I did what any gracious, understanding person would do. I laughed at him until tears rolled down my face. I may have even used the words *I told you so*. He responded by chucking a clod of dirt at me. We got into a brief dirt-clod-slinging match before he headed down the road to the farmer's house to ask him to turn off the electricity until we were finished working with the fence.

Several months later, we found ourselves working near another potentially electrified fence in a different part of the estate. When I warned him about it, he just smirked, picked up a small mud clod, and chucked it harmlessly at me. We gingerly worked around the fence and said no more about it. In his hour of potential calamity, Trevor had taken every precaution to avert injury; he had learned his lesson from a previous mistake, although thankfully not one that resulted in someone else's death, as Rumi notes.

Is life telling you to pay attention to something? Even when a thing is obvious, it's easy to think *that can't happen to me.* Funnily enough, when the obvious does happen, we're shocked—in Trevor's case, literally. Slow down and observe; take information on board and use it to make decisions. You can't prepare for every eventuality, but if you ignore warning signs, well, you see where this is going. As the British are fond of saying, what doesn't kill you makes you stronger. But I encourage you to preserve your life as much as possible.

Chapter 25

Annoyance

When people tell you that you should go to zikr and get enlightened.

Translation

Others think they know what's best for you; or no one gets you.

Rumi Verse[25]

Do not seek any rules or method of worship. Say whatever your pained heart chooses.

Unpacking It

As mentioned in Chapter 23, Braemar's courses primarily focused on the writings of the twelfth-century Muslim scholar, Sufi mystic, and philosopher Ibn Arabi. Until my arrival at Braemar, I didn't know anything about what they called the Six Month Course. On this course the students did a deep dive into Ibn Arabi's writings (among other inspired texts of various spiritual mystics). The first Braemarites I had met on a weekend reconnaissance visit kept trying to sell me on Braemar's Six Month Course, although speaking somewhat mysteriously and using unintelligible jargon. After the fourth person had strongly recommended that I take the course, or suggested that eventually I'd want to if I didn't right then, I wondered whether I had stumbled upon a cult and started looking for the exit door.

I later learned that being a student on the course involved some restrictions I wasn't prepared to submit to at the time, including an intense schedule of meditation, work, and study seven days a week for six months and without being able to leave the campus unless it was to go to the doctor or to go on the pilgrimage to Turkey—part of their coursework. I wasn't prepared for that, since part of the reason I had come to Scotland was to explore on my free time. Despite trying to make my objections clear, Braemarites continued to pressure me into doing the Six Month Course.

---

25 Helminksi and Helminski, Rumi Daylight, 146.

One night during my first week at Braemar I was watching television in the staff lounge in the manor house after supper. When the program finished, I headed downstairs to the boot hall to get my shoes and coat and return to my room in the dormitory. On my way down the front staircase, I passed the large sitting room, called the Mead Hall. Several pairs of shoes were outside the Mead Hall door. From inside the room came chanting in what I would later find out were Arabic phrases but sounded unfamiliar and odd to me at that moment. The hairs stood up on the back of my neck. What had I gotten myself into at this weird place?

Several weeks later I learned more about this nightly ritual that the students engaged in as part of the course. It was a moving meditation ritual called *zikr* (also spelled *dhikr*), which means *remembrance*, during which participants, in part, recite some of the ninety-nine names of God in the Arabic tradition. They also recite a series of repeated short prayers in deference to the Almighty. In the Christian or Judaic traditions you might think of zikr as a type of centering prayer. It is practiced by Sufis, like Rumi. Before coming to Braemar, I knew and loved Rumi's poetry but knew nothing about zikr.

When I later asked about the noises I had heard emanating from the Mead Hall, Braemarites told me that I should take the course and that I should go to zikr. Some even presumptuously implied that I wouldn't be truly enlightened until I did so. In other words, I was effectively a lost soul until I followed *their* path. These particular Braemarites weren't alone; a lot of religious believers feel this way about their particular path. None of these Braemarites, however, had any idea what my experiences or beliefs were or that I had already done a lot of spiritual soul-searching because *no one had bothered to ask me*. They didn't get me because they were too absorbed in their own viewpoint. Thankfully, it was only a handful of Braemarites who were self-righteous in this way; the majority were non-judgmental.

Eventually, I learned more about the Braemar studies and about zikr and even participated in both. After seven months there, I took their Nine Day Course, learning more about Ibn Arabi's philosophy and coming to respect it. But getting there was a challenge that required a lot of surrender, self-examination, and letting go of my own fears and judgments.

In general, I take umbrage when others tell me what they think is best for me. As long as you're a perfectly capable adult, what is best for you is between you and God. But it's impolite to tell others to faff off (as the Brits say) when they start getting preachy. It's not you, it's them, poor dears. Some people just can't help themselves when it comes to thinking they know best for everyone else. If you encounter a know-it-all you find annoying, change the subject or walk away. If you want help making choices about your life, ask a trusted person for guidance, one who won't judge but will give honest feedback. If you're so inclined, ask God for guidance, meditate, or pray. I do the latter often, and it works for me.

If *you* are one of those preachy busybodies, stop it. Although everyone is happy that you found the magic pill for living the perfect life, being in top health, making your fortune, fill in the blank, remember that your pill isn't for everyone. We were not all cut from the same tartan. Some like whisky while others prefer water. Some eat haggis while others enjoy avocado toast. People have legitimate reasons why your suggestions might not work (telling vegetarians they should go on the paleo diet, for example).

To those who believe there is only One Way to walk this Earth, I turn to Rumi: *Do not seek any rules or method of worship. Say whatever your pained heart chooses.* And I'll add, do that in whatever way brings you the most joy.

123

Chapter 26

Annoyance

When others see a drawing of your naked body.

Translation

You're embarrassed by something you did or embarrassed about who you are.

Rumi Verse[26]

Those who wear clothes look to the launderer, but the naked soul wears illumination. Either withdraw from the naked or take off your clothes like them. If you can't become wholly naked, take the middle way and take off at least some of what you wear.

Unpacking It

True confessions: Twice I modeled nude for a small art class. I knew one of the artists present, Rafi, Braemar's maintenance man. Among many other duties, he kept our temperamental generators running, or tried to when they sputtered us into darkness from time to time (see Chapter 7). He was also a skilled artist and sculptor. It was no big deal taking my clothes off in front of strangers because I thought I would never see any of them again (apart from Rafi, which was a little weird, but I dealt with it). Except I did see some of them again and we became friends. I also didn't think anyone outside the art studio would ever see the nude drawings of me. Except they did, at a public art show a few months later. By that point, my list of friends and acquaintances in my new Scotland home had swelled considerably both at Braemar and among the townsfolk. And most of them were at this art show at which a large color portrait of my naked self hung on the wall for sale.

It was all owing to my popularity that around a hundred people saw this skillfully rendered drawing at the gallery. It was hanging on the top floor in a corner, so I figured most people would miss it. I also thought that if they did see it, they wouldn't know it was me (even though the title was

---

26   Helminksi and Helminski, *Rumi Daylight*, 195.

my name), or maybe they would have too much to drink at the show to remember the next day. Here's where the popularity part comes in. It's not that I was popular among my newfound friends; I was popular with two little Braemar girls who were at the art show with their parents. They happened to discover the drawing and promptly announced it to the entire gallery, "Sarah, Sarah, we saw your naked drawing, and it looks *just* like you!"

Everyone made their way to it. Now, I'm not ashamed of my body, but I am an American. We don't typically show our nude bodies in public. I had grown close to my new Braemar friends, but did they really need to know *bare details* about me? In the end, it was all good. My fifteen minutes of fame sizzled then died with little fanfare, although the embarrassment hung around awhile. Through a serendipitously timely social media connection, I was able to buy that drawing more than twenty years later. It turned out to be a lot less revealing than I had remembered. The point is, no one teased or made fun of me nor made a big deal about it, except for me, at the time. Now I earn a little money telling that story to the world and inviting others to laugh—*with* me.

Though you may not have ever appeared nude in public, I'm sure you've experienced plenty of embarrassing episodes. Can you laugh at yourself? Are you hiding something that embarrasses you because you fear others might tease or judge? Perhaps a not-so-pretty past or an odd (but legal) hobby or pleasure? Whatever it is, there is no need to dress behind figurative clothes, the false trappings you choose to hide your true self. People who are genuine and comfortable in their own skin will accept you, warts and all. Rumi invites us to take off our figurative clothes, the layers of the ego, and instead present our illuminated, glorious souls to the world. By living a spirit-centered life instead of an ego-centered one, you will have fewer occasions to be embarrassed.

Chapter 27

Annoyance

....

When you get lost in a crowded marketplace in a foreign country.

Translation

....

You're paying attention to the wrong things or meddling when you should leave well enough alone.

Rumi Verse[27]

The way of love is not a subtle argument. The door there is devastation. Birds make great sky-circles of their freedom. How do they learn it? They fall, and falling, they're given wings.

Unpacking It

Part of the Braemar Six Month Course involved a two-week pilgrimage to Turkey, visiting the tombs of saints, sacred religious sites, and historical ruins, among other places. The trip was in December to coincide with the anniversary of Rumi's death in 1273 and included a visit to Konya, site of his tomb.

We spent a couple of days in Bursa, a picturesque mountain town with lively markets and thermal baths. Our group of forty pilgrims headed out one morning to visit the tomb of a Sufi saint who had some significance to the Braemar course. The bus dropped us off at the top end of the Grand Bazaar, which we walked through toward our destination. It seemed a long way, and the maze-like market was bustling. I didn't know where we were going nor the name of the saint whose tomb we were going to see (Hazreti Uftade, I later found out). I just tried to keep up with the group.

As the youngest of five, with a big age gap between me and the oldest, I got left out of a lot of family activities. Who wants their bratty little sister tagging along? Because of this, I'm ultra-sensitive about people being left out or left behind. Whenever I traveled in groups—I was a tour manager for a time—I played the role of chief shepherd to ensure everyone kept up. On this particular day hustling

---

27 Barks, *Birdsong*, 13.

through the bazaar in Bursa, Turkey, I noticed a couple of people in our group lagging behind. Even though it wasn't my responsibility to play tour manager on that trip, I asked a fellow traveler to go back and herd the people who weren't keeping up while I ran ahead to get a glimpse of the main group that was moving quickly through the crowded marketplace. My plan was to play the role of relay, helping to herd the laggers to our destination. Then I lost sight of everyone.

That's when it dawned on me *I had no idea where we were going nor even the name of our hotel so that I could go back*. I had no phone. I didn't speak Turkish. The realization momentarily paralyzed me. I stood in the center of the bazaar feeling utterly lost, vulnerable, and terrified. How would they find me or I them? How long before they would even notice I was missing? When I could move again, I started running down the various market alleyways searching for my people. By some miracle, several minutes later I spotted a familiar purple jacket several yards ahead. I ran to catch up.

Two things went wrong here: 1) I meddled where I shouldn't have; 2) I failed to get informed not only about our destination but about our hotel. Grabbing a hotel calling card or a matchbook on my way out the door would have solved one problem. Not relying solely on others to guide me would have solved the other. So would have minding my own business and not making false assumptions. Turns out the fellow Braemarite whom I had asked to help guide the laggers knew where we were going; I could have just stuck with him and the laggers. Though before he could tell me that, I ran off to play shepherd.

It's not that you should avoid showing concern for others, but get all the information before you act. Your concern might be misplaced or your assumptions false. I interpret Rumi's caution about the way of love leading to devastation as this: When we pursue the greatness of Love, when we choose to be better people, inevitably our familiar habits must be torn away; they are built on ego, faulty ground. But like birds testing out our ability to fly, we will falter or even plunge to the ground in changing those habits. Yet in messing up, we are also learning, we are given wings to fly. My shepherding attempt in that Turkish bazaar wasn't my first—and won't be my last—effort at meddling. But I won't ever forgot that paralyzing fear of feeling utterly lost in a strange country. Over the years I've learned to keep my nose out of things that don't concern me, although telling the ego it doesn't always know best is a lifelong practice in vigilance.

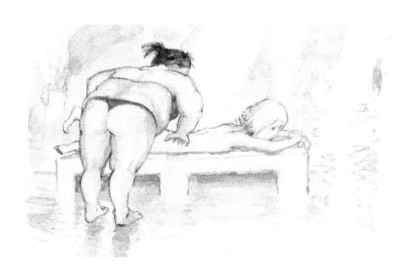

Chapter 28

....

When a large Turkish scrubbing lady is determined to break you.

Translation

....

Someone takes advantage of your vulnerability.

Rumi Verse[28]

This being human is a guest house. Every morning a new arrival. A joy, a depression, a meanness, some momentary awareness comes as an unexpected visitor. Be grateful for whoever comes, because each has been sent as a guide from beyond.

Unpacking It

As Chapter 27 noted, I was invited to go to Turkey with the students who were taking Braemar's Six Month Course. At the end of the pilgrimage, we had traveled from one end of the country to the other in all kinds of weather, but mostly cold and sometimes in freezing sleet. The weather and the hectic touring schedule prompted three women and me to seek the comforts of a traditional Turkish bath on the final night of the trip.

The four of us crammed into a cab and headed to a bathhouse recommended by our hotel. I had never had a Turkish bath; I thought it might be like a spa with hot tubs. The experience began when the four of us got naked in an anteroom. We were then led to a cavernous hall of marble walls, floors, and ceilings. Here we rinsed ourselves with warm water that came from spigots in the walls, while waiting for our scrubbing ladies. I didn't have any idea what to expect, and it was only during the scrub that I discovered the purpose was to scrape layers of skin from your body using sandpaper-like loofahs. In ten-minute intervals, a scrubbing lady would enter the cavernous hall, the bathing room, and choose one from our group to work on. I watched as each of my three companions were chosen before me. Of petite frame, I was by far the smallest of

---

28   Barks, *Essential Rumi*, 109.

us. So naturally it made sense that the last scrubbing lady to enter the bathing room, *my* scrubbing lady, was by far the largest of the four scrubbers.

The massive "treatment specialist," wearing nothing but a thong and skimpy bra, motioned for me to come lay myself down on the sacrificial marble slab in the center of the room. Here is where my companions had been moaning for the past thirty minutes from their treatments. Enjoyment or regret? I couldn't tell but suspected the latter. Trembling, I obeyed Madame.

There's something rather menacing about a person three times your size looming over your naked body while scraping off layers of your skin in sheets and barking commands: *Sit! Lie! No whimper!* Maybe it lasted three hours or just forty-five minutes, but my experience was singular in that all I could think about was surviving it. She grabbed my limbs, tugged at my toes, and practically pulled my fingers and arms out of their sockets. Maybe scrubs aren't supposed to be gentle, but at least she could have been less aggressive. She appeared to take pleasure from flipping me around like a fish on a filleting board. The scrub ended with a face and neck "massage." Madame shoved soapy fingers into my ear canals then wrenched my head back into her pumpkin-sized breasts to roughly stroke my exposed throat.

Maybe the scrubbing lady enjoyed tormenting me or maybe she just had a strong personality. Either way, being completely naked and more or less at her mercy left me feeling quite helpless. Should I have acted less afraid and demanded more respect? Should I have asked her to ease up or not show that I felt genuine pain at times? She didn't speak much English, and I no Turkish except for "thank you," which seemed an odd thing to say to someone who appeared to take advantage of my vulnerability.

We've all felt vulnerable at times, but that's not always

a bad thing (read Brené Brown). Although vulnerability has its merits, it is never okay for anyone to take advantage of or harm you. I don't think Madame had malicious intentions, although it felt like it at certain moments during my scrub. Nevertheless, I got the impression she was taking advantage of my small, exposed frame. During plenty of other times in my life it was clear people were taking advantage of me. (I'm talking to *you*, the ten-year-old who confiscated and ate a whole bag of Milk Duds fun packs that I was going to hand out to my Montessori class on my fifth birthday when you told me I wasn't allowed to!) Madame was one of a cast of many thousands who have entered and will continue to enter and leave my sphere.

As Rumi points out, life brings us all kinds of people, resulting in joy, depression, meanness, and even momentary, unexpected awareness. Be grateful for them all, for they have come to teach you something. If you pay attention, you might even figure out what that something is.

Chapter 29

Annoyance

When fog settles in the valley, and no one is allowed to speak.

Translation

You don't know what lies ahead and you can't even talk about it.

Rumi Verse[29]

A bird delegation came to Solomon complaining,
"Why is it you never criticize the nightingale?"
"Because my way," explained the nightingale for
Solomon, "is different. Mid-March to mid-June I
sing. The other nine months, while you continue
chirping, I am silent."

Unpacking It

Combined with Scotland's cool, wet weather, the hilly topography in our little corner of the country lent itself to frequent fog settling in low spots. The internal weather of our Braemar community also sometimes led to fog of the emotional kind. In other words, living in close quarters with a diversity of people—with our cultural differences, quirks, and peccadillos—sometimes got the better of us. At various times, we all griped and complained or suffered from temporary bad moods (some permanently temporary).

You've probably had the experience of someone in your living or work space being in a bad mood that then affects everyone else within stink-eye distance. At Braemar, sometimes our unresolved issues festered to the point where it became necessary for the head honcho to send us to our rooms, metaphorically speaking. On one such day, the head honcho decided to nip our gripes in the bud by declaring a day of silence. Starting after breakfast, no one was allowed to talk—at all—until breakfast the next morning. All regular business such as house cleaning, meal preparation, and outdoor estate work had to be conducted with facial expressions and gestures—the nice kind.

---

29 Barks, Birdsong, 36.

That day also happened to be one where the fog settled in so thick, it didn't clear out until the next morning. (The only place I had ever experienced something similar was at the top of a 6,800-foot ski mountain back in my home of Montana.) Visibility was only about five feet. It was eerie, quiet, and remarkably calming. The limited horizon forced us to focus on what was only directly in front of us while walking between the manor house and other buildings. You could hear the footsteps of others moving about, but you couldn't see them until you practically bumped into them. It became a purposeful, delicate dance with our fellow seekers, which was exactly the point.

By day's end, we had learned to communicate without words, replace frowns with smiles, and focus our attention on the immediate concerns of completing our work and fulfilling our basic needs of survival. Without the verbal reinforcement of complaining, our gripes subsided. In silence, we learned to listen to our better angels. We learned to communicate with our hearts. The fog served even more profoundly by forcing us to stay in the present. We literally didn't know what was ahead of us; we could only take one step at a time.

Sometimes focusing on the path directly ahead, instead of a hundred yards down the road, can have a calming effect. So can listening more than talking. Try communicating with kind gestures and expressions. Give the constant chatter a rest. There is peace and wisdom in silence as well as in staying in the present moment.

𝓒hapter 30

Annoyance
....

When thorns stick you, barbed wire snaps back at you, and you smash your fingers with a hammer.

Translation
....

It seems like everything is going wrong all in the same day.

Rumi Verse[30]

You don't have "bad" days and "good" days.
You don't sometimes feel brilliant and sometimes
dumb. There's no studying, no scholarly thinking
having to do with love, but there is a great deal of
plotting, and secret touching, and nights you can't
remember at all.

Unpacking It

Working on what was essentially a farm was hazardous to Trevor's and my health. Most days we didn't hurt ourselves—badly. Our skin was perpetually tattooed with bruises, cuts, scrapes, scratches, and the occasional sticky or staining stuff from some substance or other that didn't easily come off. Despite spending a lot of time patching poor fences to keep sheep in or out, our efforts didn't always hold up. Our garden crops sometimes failed miserably, if not killed by the weather. Floods and winds damaged things we had to then fix. Inside, the electricity went out, our water ran cold—or not at all (see Chapter 33)— just before that hot bath we had so eagerly been waiting for at the end of the day. We cut ourselves on a broken glass that dropped to the floor while rushing around the kitchen. Or burned ourselves at the stove, stubbed our toes on that danged iron foot of the oven, or accidentally lopped off a few inches of skin while chopping carrots. Sometimes setbacks just piled up one atop the other in a single day, as if bad juju was lurking everywhere.

Life, eh. If your day is turning out sucky, here are some ideas for taking a break:

---

30   Moyne and Barks, Open Secret, 13.

- Catch up on reading those magazines you get in the mail but never have time to look at.

- Go for a walk in a remote park where you're unlikely to run into other people.

- Binge watch a television series with a giant bowl of popcorn dripping with real butter and a pint of your favorite ice cream.

- Phone a friend.

- Play with a pet.

- Lie on your back and stare at the sky.

- Do a jigsaw puzzle, a crossword puzzle, or one of those math puzzles—or maybe skip the math if you're like me and numbers distress you.

- Go back to bed.

Alternatively, when you experience a series of obstacles, you'll have something to laugh about. Later. With all those hilarious stories you can tell, you might get invited to more parties. How fun is that!

As for Rumi, I think he's trying to tell us that we can label days—or whatever—as good or bad; however, doing so is pointless in the realm of Love, which he encourages us to pursue. Life just is, and sometimes it hurts. I'm not sure what he meant about the plotting and secret touching and unremembered nights, but I'll leave that up to your imagination. If you suffer from a day that is less than what you had hoped for, take a break by doing something that brings you pleasure.

Chapter 31

Annoyance

When your back goes out from hauling manure.

Translation

*You fail to see the inevitable consequences
of your actions.*

Rumi Verse[31]

Here is how a person once talked with their house. "Please, if you're ever about to collapse, let me know." One night, without a word, the house fell. "What happened to our agreement?" the person asked. The house answered, "Day and night I've been telling you with cracks and broken boards and holes appearing like mouths opening. But you kept patching and filling those with mud, so proud of your stopgap masonry. You didn't listen." This house is your body always saying, "I am leaving; I'm going soon."

Unpacking It

When Trevor assumed his duties as Braemar's estate manager (at the same time I first arrived), the Victorian walled garden had been left to fallow. His predecessor had no passion for growing vegetables and cut flowers. About the only thing that had been growing in the garden were nasturtiums, the colorfully flowered vines of which had taken over everything. One of my first garden duties was clearing the twisted tendril mess and burning piles and piles of them outside the garden wall to prevent them from reviving. We couldn't put them in the compost because the vines would have come back with a vengeance. To this day I don't like nasturtiums, although the flowers do add color and a peppery zing to salads.

Trevor liked a challenge, especially one that involved getting dirty and sweaty. He was the all-or-nothing type, so when he sank his pitchfork into something, he meant business. He was going to revive that walled garden to

---

31 Barks, The Glance, 83.

its Victorian glory days if it killed me. We'd have enough vegetables to feed the house residents for months (great, if you like eating cabbage and potatoes every day). We could save Braemar lots of money on grocery bills (and we did!). The only problem was how to store all this produce to keep it from rotting because we couldn't eat it fast enough (see Chapter 8).

Before we could achieve veggie nirvana, we had to condition the soil, which is a fancy way of saying it needed a lot of horse crap. And by "a lot," I mean a few tons. Seriously, tons! That was Trevor's opinion, anyway. Fortunately for him, there was a riding stable about twelve miles away, and Trevor had two helpers: me and Louisa, a woman who had recently arrived from Spain to volunteer in the garden.

Trevor's proposal was for Louisa and me to haul our ten-foot-long flatbed trailer with the half-ton Land Rover Defender over the moors on a winding single lane road, with dangerous curves and drop-offs (not to mention slick, sheep-poo-splattered surfaces) to the stables. Upon arrival, we would shovel as much horse poo as we could onto the trailer then drive back to Braemar on said dangerous road. Upon arrival back at Braemar we would shovel the poo off the trailer into a big pile outside the garden wall. From there we would load the poo into wheelbarrows and shift it to the garden plots, dumping, spreading, and digging it into the soil. Louisa couldn't speak English, so she couldn't object to this proposal, which I had foolishly agreed to. We made two to three trips a day to the stables. After two weeks, the flatbed trailer, Louisa, and I had had enough. The springs on the trailer had been groaning under the weight, which we ignored, until they finally broke. The vertebrae on me, which I ignored, got badly misaligned. Louisa, who hadn't complained but was in obvious pain, was glad when the broken trailer put an end to our poo-hauling days.

Though strong, I'm petite and knew better than to be lifting shovelfuls of manure above my waist onto a trailer and into wheelbarrows. I also labored in other work on the estate, so my body had been taking a beating for several months. I ignored the aches and pains, the blisters and numb hands. Why? The long story is that at that point in our relationship (which went from sort-of boss and employee to, well, *partners* of the love kind), Trevor and I were on shaky ground. I wanted to demonstrate my resilience. I wanted to please him at my own expense, which later translated into shelling out real cash for several chiropractic visits. The short story is because I'm stubborn and proud and I ignore my body when it tells me to stop.

Let's be clear: It is *never* okay to please another at your own physical or emotional expense. Pay attention to your health, act within your physical limits, and stop when you hear something crack (preferably before you hear something crack). Your body is the only vehicle you're going to get in this life so treat it with care and give it regular tune-ups. Is it really worth destroying yourself to prove a point or achieve something overly ambitious? Sometimes saying no is braver and tougher than saying yes. When your "house" gives you warning signs, heed the call. Don't patch it with stopgap masonry. If you have to wear support bandages on your wrists and ice your hands every night, you probably shouldn't be shoveling a half-ton of crap every day. Treat your body with loving kindness for years of lasting service.

After the manure-hauling ordeal, I began examining my physical limits and coming to terms with the fact that I was in my mid-thirties. My body was going to start deteriorating a lot faster as the years wore on. In the same poem quoted above, Rumi goes on to talk about a silent conversation with your soul and enjoying the orchard you planted with care. During my silent conversation, my soul told me it wasn't necessary to prove my toughness. I had already done that by packing up my life in Montana and moving to some odd community on the moors of southeast Scotland with no idea what I was getting myself into. It was time to enjoy the fruits and forget about so much labor.

Chapter 32

Annoyance

When weasels kill your baby ducks.

Translation

You feel helpless to prevent unpleasant things.

Rumi Verse[32]

No matter what plans you make, no matter what you acquire, the thief will enter from the unguarded side. Be occupied, then, with what you really value and let the thief take something less.

Unpacking It

One spring we decided to collect duck eggs to hatch ourselves (see Chapter 6), arrogantly thinking we could do a better job by assuming the role of Mother Duck. Such intervention requires responsibility, not to mention a great deal of fussing to ensure the incubator temperature and humidity adequately mimic a duck hen's feathered underside. If your eggs do hatch, suddenly the parenting desires you had previously shunned about your *own* reproduction leaves you asking *what was I thinking?* Then you realize it's relatively easy to give the little peepers back to their mothers to do the job they should have been allowed to do in the first place. That's the cool thing about raising baby creatures of the non-*Homo sapiens* variety. Change your mind? Give them back! Which is what we did with our small collection of fluffy ducklings.

However, they couldn't just be allowed to follow Mom around at the lakeside because dangerous creatures lurked nearby—weasels, foxes, the resident cat. The ducklings weren't even safe in the pens at night with the other forty adult ducks because weasels could climb the chicken-wire pens and get in through the open top. Weasels typically didn't go after the adult ducks, which is why we left the top uncovered—and also why we decided to collect the eggs in the first place to incubate rather than leave the

---

32   Helminksi and Helminski, Rumi Daylight, 141.

147

hens to raise them. So I guess our arrogance was really just a strong desire to protect any youngins.

To combat the potential weasel issue, we put our duck hens and babies in small, self-contained A-frame pens until the ducklings got bigger and stood a better chance against the big, bad world at the lakeside. The A-frames had a little hutch at one end where mom and babies cozied up at night. We closed the hutch door at night to prevent predators from getting in even though, technically, the outside portion of the A-frame, encased in chicken wire, was meant to keep them out. The hutch was an extra layer of protection. What we didn't think about was that it was pretty easy for a weasel to find the smallest of gaps where the wood frame rested on the ground. They could then crawl under to snatch a duckling. They did this in broad daylight. We did our best to make sure the frame was on solid ground without gaps, but we didn't always succeed. The ground was just too lumpy.

One night we forgot to close the hutch door after mom and babies were inside. And by "we" I mean "I," and I suffered horrible guilt for weeks after. A weasel or two had a field day, leaving a bloody scene and a cowering mother surrounded by one dead baby; the other three babies were gone and presumed eaten. That horror tableau still haunts me. I wanted someone to send me to the desert for forty days with a hair shirt and a whip for self-flagellation, that's how bad I felt. We lost about ten ducklings to weasels—the thieves at our unguarded door—but the weasel thieves were just doing what weasels do. It was my job to protect the ducklings, and I failed.

In my interpretation of this Rumi caution, sometimes you win and sometimes you lose. The weasels had to eat too. If there weren't fluffy ducklings, how would fluffy weasel kits survive? I eventually accepted our losses as nature's necessity and learned to take better stock of what

I valued. In this case, it was better to leave mamma ducks to raise and worry about their own babies rather than intervene. What in your life needs protecting and what can you afford to lose? Keep in mind that no matter how much you try to prevent your losses, they will always be part of your life; therefore, protect what you truly value and accept that you won't be able to protect everything.

Chapter 33

Annoyance

When the well dries up and you have to haul your own water just to flush the toilet.

Translation

Major league disruptions put a serious crimp in your daily life.

Rumi Verse[33]

Be warm, you who are cool, that heat may bear
difficulties, that ease may come.

Unpacking It

Braemar's water supply came from a 700,000-gallon spring-fed water tank buried up on the moors. The water flowed through about a mile's worth of Victorian-era iron pipe from this underground tank to the estate buildings. One evening in late November we suddenly didn't have any water despite that it had been raining nearly every day for weeks on end. But that's not how water storage works. Just because it's raining on the outside doesn't mean your reservoir is full. The shortage may have resulted from watering the heck out of the garden that summer and autumn because Trevor had tripled the planting area because, you know, you can't ever have enough potatoes (see Chapter 8). Braemar also had double the number of residents that year, so demand was high for domestic activities as well.

The water source, the spring, hadn't been able to keep up with the heavy demand. But the spring did have a backup: a pump down the hill that moved water from the stream to supplement the tank during the dry months. In Scotland, the "dry months" are when it rains only five days a week instead of seven. Apparently—though not to Trevor and me—this pump was supposed to be turned on during the summer. The people who knew about these things no longer lived at Braemar and forgot to pass along this bit of information to the new estate team (me and Trevor). So who woulda thunk that the well would dry

---

33 Helminksi and Helminski, Rumi Daylight, 171.

up when it had been dumping rain for weeks? There we were, the night before Thanksgiving, and not a drop of water. We were expecting around sixty people for the next day's big meal (no, it's not a Scottish holiday; just one that Americans brought to Braemar).

A 700,000-gallon tank doesn't just fill itself up overnight, especially when the spring trickles at the pace of a garden hose. And when you have a houseful of forty people, water is in fairly high demand. While waiting eleven days for the tank to fill, we had to haul our own water to eat, drink, wash cooking implements and dishes, bathe, and flush toilets every day. Trevor spent those eleven days driving back and forth between neighboring farmers' spigots with four 500-gallon portable tanks towed behind the tractor. At the spigots, he filled each tank with a hose, one by one. I spent those eleven days figuring out how to get the water flowing again through the pipe once the tank did fill. Water doesn't just magically start flowing again on its own (see Chapter 17). Our case involved valves and forcing water back into the pipes and all manner of coordination and trial and error, which is too complicated to explain for the purposes of this book. Everyone else spent those eleven days hauling buckets of water to bathrooms and the kitchen. It was a major disruption, to say the least. Tempers flared. My fellow water diviners and I argued about the best way to get it flowing again. We also all banded together and tried to make the best of it. We had no choice.

You never expect the well to dry up or a loved one, or yourself, to have an accident or illness or other crisis. Sometimes major disruptions happen that you have no control over, such as natural disasters or global pandemics. Some situations may be preventable if you take precautions or pay better attention, such as checking the water level. Be vigilant without being paranoid. Take care of the things you have control over so that when disruption strikes, you are better able to handle it.

For me, Rumi's suggestion to be warm, you who are cool, means stick together during a crisis; help one another and look out for those who need additional support. That heat, the warmth of human kindness, will help you bear difficulties, making way for ease. Not necessarily instant relief, but ease.

Chapter 34

Annoyance

When you try to serve American-style tea
to the British.

Translation

*Failing to accommodate others' needs lands
you in hot water.*

Rumi Verse[34]

> *If your knowledge of fire has been turned to certainty by words alone, then seek to be cooked by the fire itself. Don't abide in borrowed certainty. There is no real certainty until you burn; if you wish for this, sit down in the fire.*

Unpacking It

For a refresher on the tree planting project (what initially brought me to Braemar) and some background information on ensuring that the volunteer planters were kept fed and watered, see chapters 18 and 19. Respectively, the lessons there are 1) others will let you down, so have a backup plan, and 2) don't get your knickers in a knot about trivial matters. I could say the lesson in this chapter is that you get what you ask for, but that would be the little me—not the Big Me—talking; the Big Me being the kinder, gentler, wiser one.

During a few days of the tree event's peak attendance, about seventy volunteer planters were at Braemar at the same time out of more than one hundred total who participated over the course of two weeks. Having them all trudge into the manor house for a sit-down lunch and supper would have put a strain on the kitchen and house staff. So to accommodate the volunteers, we set up a huge army tent with a makeshift kitchen in the parking lot of the old sawmill. The mill was somewhat centrally located among the different tracts on the estate where we were planting the trees. We borrowed the tent from the local Boy Scouts, along with folding tables, Bakelite dishes, flatware, plastic cups, and a five-gallon water boiler fueled with propane.

---

34 Helminksi and Helminski, Rumi Daylight, 118.

Our chairs were wooden planks propped up with log rounds. All in all, it was a pretty comfortable camp setup. The kitchen staff would prepare our hot lunch and drive the food to the tent. We would wash the dishes there.

We also prepared the tea and coffee at the tent for our morning and afternoon breaks. One particular cold, damp day I got the tree planters started at the far end of the estate then trudged a quarter mile back to the tent to light the water boiler. It would take an hour to heat the water for that morning's tea break, so the boiler had to be lit as soon as the day started. I left the boiler to do its thing and trudged back to the tree planting site. When it came time to make the tea, I hiked back to the tent only to find the water was hottish but not quite boiling. Let me just take a second to describe how the British like their tea: boiling. How do Americans like their tea? Whatever. The morning break was nearly upon us, and there was no time to wait for the water to boil. So, like any American would do, I went with the so-so hot water temperature.

That was my first mistake. My second mistake was that there were only a half-dozen tea bags at the tent; not anywhere near enough to make what the British would consider a decent cuppa. With the break looming, and hungry, thirsty planters expecting to be satiated soon, there was no time to run back to the manor house for more tea bags. So, like any American would do, I used six tea bags for about three gallons of water when it required a couple dozen or so. I poured the tea into flasks and gathered all the goodies in boxes. Two volunteers came to the tent to carry the goods out to the tree planters. I stayed behind to start more water boiling to wash the upcoming lunch dishes.

Fifteen minutes later, a tree planter emissary appeared at the tent to talk tea. Speaking on behalf of the volunteer corps, she wanted to know whether I had mistakenly put used dishwater into the flasks instead of tea. I confessed my sins about the lukewarm water and the six tea bags per three gallons of water, and she nodded in that way one does when the light dawns and they realize they're dealing with an ignoramus. She asked whether I minded if she made more tea. Unfortunately, there wasn't *any* even warmish water now because I had used it all and only just set the boiler on with another five gallons of cold water. It would take an hour at least to heat.

That's when I started to cry. The problem went deeper than just my failure to do the right thing, I told her. The problem was that I had a lot of other more important things to do, such as make sure all the trees were getting in the ground properly so that we would get the grant money for planting the trees. For those ten days so far of planting, I had taken on too many roles, including having to sort out tea breaks because no one would volunteer for this job (see Chapter 18; this is where *you get what you ask for* comes in). The emissary put her arm around me and promised to take care of everything herself as long as I promised never to make tea again. All things considered, that was a pretty good deal.

Still, I could have done better. Knowing full well how the British like their tea, I should have taken the extra time to run to the house for more bags and waited for the water to boil before brewing substandard refreshment for volunteers who were working their tails off and deserved proper tea. They would have been willing to wait the extra time if the alternative was suffering through lukewarm water tinged brown. As the manager of the project, it was my responsibility to ensure the volunteers' needs were met. Also, I knew better than *not* to adapt to British tea-making rules.

Are the demands of others too much for you? Or maybe it's you that needs to adapt to someone else's ways?

Examine this carefully to ensure you are meeting others at least halfway. They will appreciate your efforts to "speak their language" and you might not only learn something, but make some allies along the way.

I like the obscurity of Rumi's poem. In the case of the British tea fiasco, I had knowledge that I refused to use. You could say I was certain the volunteers wouldn't call me out on the substandard tea. I was wrong; my certainty was borrowed from past events where I had failed to deliver quality yet the recipient didn't call me out. I had gotten away with it. I needed that firm but gentle reprimand from the emissary so that I could be cooked in the fire of knowledge itself and learn that adaption, when it doesn't involve compromising your values or dignity, is worth the effort, even if only to earn respect.

Chapter 35

Annoyance
....

When your car breaks down in the castle parking lot.

Translation
....

You fail to address the underlying cause of a problem.

Rumi Verse[35]

Unpacking It

About a week into the tree planting event (see chapters 18, 19, and 34), I needed a break from coordinating all the logistics and ensuring volunteers and house staff alike had what they needed. In all candor, after having a meltdown one evening after supper (one of a few meltdowns), I was *ordered* to take a day off. My sister Mary Linn and her friend Jen had come to Scotland to volunteer at the tree planting, so taking some time off allowed us to spend a day touring a few local sites. I had to borrow a car from one of the Braemarite staff. The only problem was the car was a wreck (so was I at that point, so the car and I were like soulmates). The owner hadn't driven the Blue Beast in a long time, leaving it to rot in the weather.

Braemar's maintenance man, Rafi, who had driven the car most recently, warned me not to take it. The engine was shot and various hoses were practically like Swiss cheese. He was good with all things mechanical, which meant I probably should have listened to him. But I really needed to get away for the day and no one else was willing to lend me their car. Rafi was between vehicles, or he would have lent his. After seeing my determination, he gave it a good once-over to make sure all the bits and bobs were in place and the thing had fresh oil. He even replaced one of the hoses. At least if the Blue Beast broke down, it

---

35 Turkmen, Rumi's Masnevi, 116-117.

160

would have clean underwear, so to speak.

As Mary Linn, Jen, and I were getting into the car that morning of our release from tree planting duties, Rafi warned me once more. I didn't listen. For the first hour or so the Blue Beast was mostly fine; a few coughs and sputters, a minor head cold. We stopped at a historic site to explore before heading to Floors Castle, which was this great pile of ancient building blocks housing the current Duke of Roxburgh and his family. Like most British people with inherited titles and a massive manor house to go with it, the Duke opened a small part of his home to tourists to help pay the electric bills. Being nosy and envious Americans, we wanted to see how that 0.01 percent lived. When we pulled into the castle parking lot, the car started coughing and sputtering more and then steam seeped from under the hood. The head cold had turned into pneumonia.

I called Rafi from the phone in the parking lot attendant's booth. Not being the type to rub it in, Rafi didn't say "see, I told you so." Instead, he said, "I was afraid this was going to happen. Why didn't you listen to me?" After the scolding, he told me to let the car cool down then pour water into the radiator and head straight back to Braemar before we got ourselves into more trouble.

We toured the castle while the engine settled then attempted to revive our patient. To get water in the radiator, we fished plastic water bottles out of the parking lot trash can and filled them in the public restrooms. The car wouldn't start, so my sister—an expert at pop-starting stick shift junk vehicles—got behind the wheel. Jen and I pushed the Blue Beast up the little incline in the parking lot. Several people stood by and watched, not offering to help. Finally the thing started, and we were on our way. And we were hungry, so we stopped for fish and chips. On the way to the chip shop, more steam poured from under the hood. I could barely see the road ahead. After our meal, the car wouldn't start again. Enter pop-starting, fiercely cussing sister to the rescue.

Eventually, we made it to Eltondean, the town nearest Braemar, where Rafi rescued us in the estate Land Rover, which we used to tow the Blue Beast. It was the most adventurous relaxing day off I had ever had! In retrospect, by taking the Blue Beast out that day, we could have had or caused a car crash. We could have totally broken down in the boonies miles from help or a phone (I didn't own a cell phone back then).

Likewise you may not like to hear about broken things, especially if they might disrupt your plans. Rumi tells us to act before our stress becomes chains binding us and before warnings in our heart prevent us from moving in the right direction. Have you ever chosen to ignore what you don't want to know about? It's easy to do if your emotional state is suffering, like mine was at the time. You might think everything will be fine or breakdowns won't happen to you. If the warning lights are flashing—or a trustworthy person clearly warns you—pay attention. If possible, fix what's broken or change plans or abandon course; a car, a relationship, a job. Don't put yourself or others at risk. Take all warnings seriously.

Chapter 36

Annoyance

When you walk for days in the rain and wonder whether you'll ever reach your destination.

Translation

You question whether your big goals are worth the effort.

Rumi Verse[36]

You try to accomplish things, to win, to reach goals. This is not the true situation. Put the whole world in ambition's stomach, it'll never be enough. Assume you get everything you want. Assume you have it now. What's the point? The next moment you die. Friend, the youth you've lived is ending. You sleep a drunken dreamless sleep with no sense what morning you could wake inside.

Unpacking It

Toward the end of my Braemar experience I decided to do a walking pilgrimage. It wasn't enough that I had spent eighteen months of my life essentially on a pilgrimage. My friend Jill first told me about the sixty-two-mile path called St. Cuthbert's Way. Initially, we decided to walk it together, but health concerns forced her to back out. So I ended up walking The Way by myself for six days.

Trevor had impressed upon me that it was important to walk *every inch* of the journey; no cheating. During the first two days, the starting and stopping points were close enough to home that he could pick me up and bring me home, which meant I could get a hot bath and sleep in my own bed. When Trevor dropped me off at the trailheads those first couple of days, he drove me to the *exact same spot* where he picked me up the day before. He spared no mercy, refusing to drive me farther down the road to give me a head start. He even made me get out of the car to start day three in the rain. He claimed I would hate myself if I didn't suffer through every inch of The Way, weather be damned. I didn't think I would hate myself, but he had

---

36 Barks, The Glance, 86.

the car keys. For the last three nights, I carried everything I needed in a backpack and stayed in hostels.

Walking from Melrose, Scotland, to Lindisfarne, England (a.k.a., Holy Isle), I averaged about twelve miles a day. I walked, climbed, and sometimes staggered with aching legs across a varied landscape, from flat, grassy paths along riverbanks to the rugged Cheviot Mountains. Mostly, the path coursed through rolling countryside, up and down, up and down. In other words, it was no walk in the park but it also wasn't a Himalayan trek. I had done some solo traveling before but never walked so far for an entire week alone.

To get the best chance of sunshine, I chose to do the pilgrimage in early May, typically a dry month in that part of Scotland. It still rained. And rained. And rained. For five days the skies spit, showered, or dumped on me.

Day four was the most difficult: hiking up and over the Cheviot Mountains and no towns along the way to stop for a meal (I carried trail mix and an apple in my pack). The morning of that hike the skies were dumping it down. The rain lashed sideways. I waited in the hostel for an hour in case it stopped. An older lady I had met there offered me a ride to my next destination to spare me having to hike in the monsoon. I was tempted. Yet after having come so far, suffering through the weather, tough terrain, and periodic loneliness, I thought, *What would Trevor do?* The answer was clear: he would never let me forget that I had cheated by cutting out a full thirteen miles. "But how is he to know?" the lady posited, adding, "No sense in catching your death just to please a man." Forsooth, the temptress had been sent by the Devil himself!

Despite her logical argument, I declined the offer and headed out to face the day's journey. It poured nearly the entire eight-hour day, which didn't matter much because within ten minutes of first starting out, my "waterproof" jacket and over-trousers leaked. Within the first thirty minutes I was drenched and remained so the rest of the day. The seams on my boots began to rot, bathing my feet. My skin turned ghostly and wrinkled. To retain my sanity, I focused on each step, not how far I had to go. I talked to the sheep and cows I encountered. I cursed not only the weather gods but Trevor. I wondered whether I would be able to finish, to reach my destination without getting lost in the difficult terrain. Or would I collapse on the mountain and become vulture food? What was I thinking doing this on my own?

Nah. At day's end, the rain stopped and I had made it. That night I ate a hot pub meal with a half-pint of stout and slept in a dry, warm bed in a nice hostel. I was further rewarded on day five with clear, sunny skies and no rain, although I did get sunburned. Jill met me on day six to walk the final mile across the sands to Lindisfarne when the tide was out. When she and I reached the shore, we embraced and I cried. I had actually finished! Trevor was right: I would have regretted not walking every step, taking the easy way out on that Cheviot day. I was proud of myself for sticking it out despite the doubts and blisters. After all, this was a pilgrimage, the point of which was to build strength for weathering life.

Sometimes it's tempting to give up your goal when you're faced with unpleasantries. During the difficult times, try focusing on the steps—the minutia—rather than looking at the looming mountain and wondering how you're going to make it to the top. When things get tough, it's natural to question whether we've made the right choice. *Should I be doing this? Surely something I want so badly shouldn't be this difficult! Why am I doing this?*

The bigger the goal, the more crap you have to push through to reach it. Don't give up if the goal is worth fighting for; you may live to regret it. On the other hand, *are* your goals worth it? *Assume you get everything you want. Assume you have it now. What's the point? The next moment you die.* Rumi's words sound harsh, yet I think he cautions us not to get too caught up in reaching goals, striving for ambitions for ambition's sake. It's not just about the goal; it's about what we gain along the way. No, not soggy feet and wrinkled skin but rather the strength to keep going despite being weary and wet. My pilgrimage was a metaphor for life: There are moments of solitude and of companionship; sun and rain, wind and sleet; starting out and reaching the end; and the sublime joy of accomplishing something ambitious yet totally worth plowing ahead for.

Chapter 37

Annoyance

When you have to remove pictures from the wall because they are weird.

Translation

Another religion, lifestyle, culture, race, fill-in-the-blank feels threatening.

Rumi Verse[37]

All religions, all this singing, one song. The differences are just illusion and vanity. The sun's light looks a little different on this wall than it does on that wall. And a lot different on this other one, but it's still one light.

Unpacking It

When I first arrived at Braemar one of the things that caught my eye most notably was the presence of a certain style of picture hanging on the wall in every room of the manor house and the dormitory. They were Arabic calligraphies beautifully rendered in pen and ink, with colorful flourishes and designs in the margins. They reminded me of the illuminated manuscripts of the Bible drawn by early, super-dedicated monks. You have to admire a person who spent his life in a cold, dark monastery eating gruel and stale bread and creating these amazing works of art by candlelight out of ink and tanned sheep hide. I loved the artistry of such works from the Bible, a book with which I have some familiarity having been brought up in the Christian tradition.

These Arabic works of art basically fell into a similar category in that they glorified God. But it wasn't *my* religion; it was Islam, which I knew nothing about, and I was raised in a culture that didn't think respectful things about it either (not my parents, just my culture). My ignorance made me believe that Braemar's calligraphies were somehow sacrilegious—which is funny because I wasn't strict about religion of any kind. Not knowing anything about it, I took down the picture from above my bed and stuffed

---

37   Green, One Song, 28.

it under some clothes in my dresser drawer. I couldn't be bothered to ask anyone about it either, having assumed everyone at Braemar was a converted Muslim and would try to convert me, or worse, put a curse on me for removing the picture. See how ignorance and stubbornness can lead one down an unfriendly path?

Spoiler alert: Braemarites weren't converted Muslims, and even if they were, it would have been fine. Braemar was not a religious retreat; it did not espouse any one path but rather focused on the nature of God, who transcends human-made religion. Over time, my exposure to just a taste of Islam and associated inspired writings broadened my understanding of the religion and, therefore, my comfort with the iconography scattered about Braemar. Eventually, I got the nerve to ask someone the meaning of the Arabic calligraphies and learned they were prayers of protection. I fished the picture out of my drawer and hung it back over my bed where it belonged. And I'm still here to tell the tale.

If you find "other" threatening, ask yourself why. Is it truly a threat or does it just feel uncomfortable because it is outside your understanding or experience? Make an effort to understand other things and people who are different from you. Read books or attend cultural festivals or worship ceremonies of a practice outside your own. (God won't think you're a heretic.) If you belong to a spiritual community, invite someone from another community to speak to yours about their beliefs.

Ask people whom you might label as "other" polite questions and with a genuine desire to understand, not in an interrogating or judgmental way. Oftentimes people who are approached with sincere curiosity will be flattered that you care and will happily share with you. Some maybe not so much. Race and religion have become sensitive topics in our culture, so people may see the questions themselves as a threat or feel like they shouldn't have to "explain" themselves to others. Regardless whether people get offended or share with you, accept their response gracefully and thank them. Avoid offering your opinion or beliefs in exchange unless they ask you to share.

Try seeing differences as a gift rather than a barrier to acceptance. A little kindness, consideration, and compassion to others we don't normally interact with go a long way in creating positive relationships among our global community. As Rumi says, all religions can be reduced to all of us singing one song—that is, praising God. The differences are just illusion and vanity. But it's not just religion; it's culture, the illusion of race, the country we come from, the music or books we prefer, the jobs we do. These are just the clothes of being human that decorate the outer self. Inside we are all one light.

Chapter 38

Annoyance

....

When God lets you down.

Translation

....

The one force you should be able to count on abandons you.

Rumi Verse[38]

Each moment contains a hundred messages from God. To every cry of "Oh, Lord!" He answers a hundred times, "I am here."

Unpacking It

Though the memory is vague, I can recall the time when I first declared I didn't believe in God. I was nine or ten years old and began questioning the existence of something that couldn't be seen, felt, tasted, heard, or smelled (so I thought). Mom was the recipient of this announcement and, unflinching, responded that *she* believed in God, and it didn't matter that I doubted because God loved me anyway. I don't remember what else she said, but I remember her gentle reaction. I'm sure she thought I would come around some day. She was right, of course. However, many years passed before I fully learned to appreciate the nature of God, eventually leading me to understand that I don't know Jack Crap about the Almighty. But that doesn't mean I can't have a decent relationship with Her.

I come from a family of Presbyterian preachers, so it was more or less expected of us to accept God. A little questioning was encouraged, but my parents raised us as Christians and hoped we would all continue to be Christians as adults. For the record, I haven't belonged to a church for many years, although I attend different ones periodically. When I left home for college I continued to go to church for a couple of years. Eventually, church began to feel more ritualistic than spiritually fulfilling. Besides, it ate into my Sunday morning free time, so I stopped going. It wasn't that I had a problem with God, I just couldn't

---

38 Helminksi and Helminski, Rumi Daylight, 43.

feel the strong relationship I had expected. Chalk it up to indifference or ignorance or a little of both. For whatever reason I just wasn't feeling compelled.

Over the years I explored different ways of connecting to a supreme force, mostly through what is sometimes pejoratively referred to as New Age practices: books, meditation gatherings, lectures, physio-spiritual healing (I just made up that term), whatever came my way via encountered kindred souls. I even hung out with Buddhists for a while. These experiences began to strengthen my belief in, and relationship with, the universal force I choose to call God. They also strengthened my conviction that there is no single True Religion. That doesn't mean everybody is wrong; it actually means everybody is right! Everyone is free to practice the spiritual path of their choosing without fear of going to Hell. You may disagree, but that doesn't make either of us wrong. In my view, it demonstrates the beauty of the Divine, who loves us all so much that She doesn't care that you call yourself a Snexle and I call myself a Hooliewoo. Or that you worship ten times a day and I worship once a week. Or that you prefer to get your divine inspiration from Person X and I prefer it from Person Q.

Regardless of your chosen path, being filled with the love and presence of God feels brilliant! Until it doesn't. If you don't have a Person X or a Person Q for inspiration, or even believe in a divine universal force, I hope you have at least experienced elation or felt deeply loved by another. So we don't always walk around feeling fantastic. Sometimes life sucks. Sometimes a lot of times.

I went through a phase of having what I thought was a pretty good understanding between me and God. She took care of my needs, and I was grateful and tried to be a good person. Then things weren't so great in my opinion. My life felt like a dead-end deal. I started blaming God for it. If She wasn't going to fix it, I was going to turn my life around by quitting my job, selling my house, and leaving the country. It actually worked. Eventually. But not necessarily because I quit my job, sold my house, and left the country for Scotland. It worked because I hit rock bottom emotionally before realizing my life was my responsibility. Actually, I hit bottom several times, but it was my time at Braemar that lit the fire under me, lifted me up.

Life got better, not because life got better—that is, everything was pretty much the same—but because I changed my attitude about it. I started seeing things differently; responding instead of reacting. I also developed a deeper affection for God. Then things got sucky again, then better, then . . . well, you get the picture. But the bad times were easier to weather because I knew it was my response to them that made the difference in my experience of them. It wasn't God pulling strings or dumping on me. God was just there saying, "Look, if you want help, I'm here. But you gotta take responsibility for your own thoughts and deeds. So whatta ya gonna do about it?"

If you're like me, you've done a lot of crying to or bitching at God. And when that doesn't work, you try bargaining. But have you tried taking responsibility? God hasn't really let you down; She just has more faith in you than you do. Parents have to let their children fall so they can learn how to get back up. God can guide you but She isn't going to take over and make your life all rainbows and unicorns—or rain clouds and dragons. You reap what you sow (*karma* in the Buddhist tradition). So put on your big-person pants and start doing the heavy lifting.

We're here to enjoy this stunning world, to experience joy and love and laughter. The yucky things remind us to be grateful for the nice things and also remind us that with enough will—and sometimes hard work—we have the power to slay the yucky things. This is what I began to learn during my experience at Braemar. Before leaving

Montana to make that long journey, I had begged God to improve my dead-end life. She sent me to a small corner of Scotland, on the verge of despair yet armed with determination and a few Rumi poems in my heart.

If light is in your heart, you will find your way home.

Bibliography

All poems are by Jelal ad-Din Rumi. The authors listed herein are translators of Rumi's works.

AZquotes. Rumi. https://www.azquotes.com.

Barks, Coleman. *Rumi Birdsong: Fifty-three Short Poems.* Athens, GA: Maypop, 1993.

———. *The Essential Rumi.* 2nd ed. Edison, NJ: Castle Books, 1997.

———. *The Glance: Songs of Soul-Meeting.* 2nd ed. New York: Penguin Compass, 2001.

———. *The Soul of Rumi: A New Collection of Ecstatic Poems.* New York: HarperSanFrancisco, 2002.

Green, Michael. *One Song: A New Illuminated Rumi.* Philadelphia: Running Press, 2005.

Helminski, Camille and Kabir Helminski. *Rumi Daylight: A Daybook of Spiritual Guidance.* 3rd ed. Putney, VT: Threshold Books, 1994.

Helminski, Kabir, ed. *The Pocket Rumi.* Boulder, CO: Shambhala, 2008.

Khalili, Nader. *The Spiritual Poems of Rumi.* New York: Wellfleet Press, 2018.

Moyne, John and Coleman Barks. *Open Secret: Versions of Rumi.* Putney, VT: Threshold Books, 1984.

———. *Say I Am You: Poetry Interspersed with Stories of Rumi and Shams.* Athens, GA: Maypop, 1994.

Türkmen, Erkan. *The Essence of Rumi's Masnevi Including His Life and Works.* Konya, Turkey: Misket, 1992.

Acknowledgments

Anne Dubuisson for editing (AnneConsults.com) and Nevin Mays (nevinmays.com) for copyediting. Kolleen Kidd (author, *A Rose for Sergei*), Julie Seely (author, *Skinny House*), and Shabnam Curtis (author, *My Persian Paradox*) for manuscript feedback. Philip Gulley (author, *Unlearning God: How Unbelieving Helped Me Believe* and numerous other books) for the lovely advanced review. Ori Soltes (author, *Mysticism in Judaism, Christianity, and Islam: Searching for Oneness*) for his advanced review and the beautiful Foreword, as well as help with Rumi resources. Ibrahim Anli, executive director of the Rumi Forum, Sara Towe Horsfall, and Zeki Saritoprak (author, *Islam's Jesus*) for their advanced reviews and help with Rumi resources. Michelle Argyle for the book design (Melissa Williams Design). Simon Blackwood for the charming illustrations.

Author Bio

S.A. Snyder has worn hats as a writer, editor, reporter and columnist, writing instructor, and communications consultant. In a previous life she was a forester and wildlife biologist. Her experience covers topics as diverse as environmental sciences, electrical and mechanical engineering, telecommunications, travel marketing, finance and insurance, adaptive recreation, health and wellness, workplace safety and security, and general business. Sarah's latest adventures include oral storytelling, public speaking, and inspiring others to discover their true potential.

Also by S.A. Snyder

Plant Trees, Carry Sheep: A Woman's Spiritual Journey
Among the Sufis of Scotland
(Luna River Publishing, 2019)

Scenic Driving Montana
(4th edition, Rowman & Littlefield, 2021)

Forthcoming by S.A. Snyder

Non-Fiction

Hu Let the Sheep Out:
Life Lessons from Animals I've Known

DIY Retreats: How to Create the Self-Care You Need

Fiction

Aislinn Zafirah Trilogy

In this comedy of errors, an animal rights activist must
help her reincarnated, beastly, mother solve the
mystery of her death.

Luna River

A tragic story of mother and child, loss and redemption,
set in Wyoming.

Connect with S.A. Snyder

Visit www.lunarivervoices.com to:

- Sign up for the newsletter
- Download book club discussion questions
- Watch YouTube videos of Sarah's live storytelling
- Take a quick quiz to determine whether you're ready for your own retreat or adventure
- Prepare for your retreat or adventure
- Learn more about the Sufi poet Jelal ad-Din Rumi
- Find links to retreats and more

Facebook: S.A. Snyder

Twitter: @LunaRiverVoices

Instagram: @s.a.snyder

To book S.A. Snyder for speaking, storytelling, or reading engagements, visit www.LunaRiverPublishing.com.

I invite you to post a book review on Amazon or your favorite book website.